Civilization, Culture and Development of Ancient India

PAWAN KUMAR SINGH

ISBN:

TO MY DEAREST PARENTS

The book is dedicated to my parents with all my love and gratitude. Their unwavering support, wisdom, and belief in me is a great source of my strength always.

CONTENTS

ACKNOWLEDGMENTS

I would like to express my deepest gratitude to everyone who contributed to the creation of this work on Ancient Indian culture and Civilization. First, I am profoundly thankful to my mentors and colleagues for their insightful guidance and encouragement throughout this journey. Their expertise in history, philosophy, and the arts greatly enriched the content of this book.

I also extend my appreciation to the various scholars whose research and writings served as foundational sources, providing the intellectual framework for this study. Special thanks go to my family and friends for their unwavering support, patience, and understanding during the many hours of research and writing.

Chapter 1

Introduction to Ancient Indian Culture and Civilization

Ancient Indian culture and civilization, spanning millennia, is a rich tapestry of diverse traditions, beliefs, and achievements. Rooted in the Indus Valley Civilization, one of the world's oldest urban societies, it evolved through various epochs. Vedic literature, composed around 1500-500 BCE, laid the foundation for Hinduism, influencing art, philosophy, and social norms. Buddhism, founded by Siddhartha Gautama, emerged in the 6th century BCE as a major philosophical and spiritual movement. The Maurya and Gupta Empires witnessed advances in science, mathematics, and art. India's multiculturalism fostered Jainism, Sikhism, and the assimilation of foreign cultures. This cultural heritage, encompassing music, dance, yoga, and more, continues to shape modern India.

Meaning of Culture

Culture refers to the collective set of shared beliefs, values, customs, traditions, behaviors, and artifacts that characterize a particular group of people, society, or community. It encompasses the way people think, communicate, interact, and express themselves, as well as the practices and rituals that define their identity. Culture plays a crucial role in shaping individuals' perspectives and behaviors, guiding social norms and relationships, and influencing various aspects of life, such as art, religion, language, cuisine, and social structures. It is a dynamic and evolving concept, reflecting the evolving nature of human societies and their interactions with the world.

Culture has been defined by various authors and scholars, each offering their unique perspectives. Here are a few notable definitions:

1. Edward B. Tylor (1871): Tylor, often considered a founding figure in anthropology, defined culture as "that complex whole which includes knowledge, belief, art, morals, law, custom, and any other capabilities and habits acquired by man as a member of society."

2. Clifford Geertz (1973): Geertz, an influential cultural anthropologist, described culture as "a system of inherited conceptions expressed in symbolic forms by means of which men communicate, perpetuate, and develop their knowledge about and attitudes toward life."

3. Ruth Benedict (1934): Benedict, another prominent anthropologist, offered a more concise definition, calling culture "a set of shared understandings that people learn through the process of socialization."

4. E.B. Tylor (1871): Tylor also proposed a simpler definition: "Culture or civilization, taken in its wide ethnographic sense, is that complex whole which includes knowledge, belief, art, morals, law, custom, and any other capabilities and habits acquired by man as a member of society."

5. Kroeber and Kluckhohn (1952): These anthropologists described culture as "patterns, explicit and implicit, of and for behavior acquired and transmitted by symbols, constituting the distinctive achievements of human groups, including their embodiments in artifacts."

Indian authors have also contributed to the understanding of culture in various ways. Here are a couple of definitions by Indian authors:

1. R.K. Mukherjee: He defined culture as "the totality of beliefs, values, customs, institutions, art, technology, and social behavior of a social group."

2. M.N. Srinivas: A renowned Indian sociologist, Srinivas described culture as "a complex whole which includes knowledge, beliefs, art, morals, laws, customs, and other capabilities and habits acquired by man as a member of society."

These definitions by Indian authors align with the broader understanding of culture as a comprehensive system of beliefs, values, and practices that characterize a particular society or community. They emphasize the multifaceted nature of culture and its significance in shaping human behavior and societies. These definitions reflect the multidimensional and complex nature of culture, emphasizing its role in shaping human societies and individual identities.

Indian authors also have contributed significantly to the study of culture, reflecting the country's diverse heritage. Culture in India is often described as a mosaic of traditions, languages, religions, and customs. Indian sociologist Geetanjali Pandit defines culture as "the soul of a society," emphasizing its spiritual and profound influence on people's lives. Diverse definitions abound, reflecting India's multicultural tapestry. Scholars like S.C. Dubey and Kapila Vatsyayan have delved into the nuances of Indian culture, highlighting its dynamic nature. Overall, these Indian perspectives underscore the richness of culture in India, characterized by its deep-rooted traditions, cultural pluralism, and enduring spirituality.

Meaning of Civilization

Civilization, a complex and multifaceted concept, encompasses the pinnacle of human societal development. It denotes an advanced stage of human organization, marked by distinct characteristics, achievements, and cultural elements. Here's an in-depth exploration of the meaning of civilization:

1. Social Organization: Civilization is characterized by a structured social order. It involves the establishment of governments, laws, and hierarchies that regulate interactions within a society. This organization enables the efficient allocation of resources, division of labor, and the maintenance of order.

2. Economic Systems: Civilizations often develop sophisticated economic systems. These systems may include agriculture, trade, and industry. The ability to produce surplus food and goods allows for the growth of urban centers and specialization of labor.

3. Technological Advancements: Advancements in technology are a hallmark of civilization. These innovations encompass a wide range of fields, from agriculture and transportation to communication and medicine. Technological progress enhances the quality of life and enables societies to tackle complex challenges.

4. Cultural Achievements: Civilizations produce a rich tapestry of cultural achievements. This includes art, literature, music, architecture, and religious practices. Cultural expression reflects the values, beliefs, and creativity of a society.

5. Urbanization: Civilizations are often associated with the development of cities and urban centers. Urbanization results from population growth, economic specialization, and the need for centralized administration. Cities become hubs of culture, commerce, and governance.

6. Writing and Record-Keeping: Many civilizations develop writing systems to document their history, laws, and knowledge. Writing facilitates communication across time and space and allows for the preservation of cultural heritage.

7. Religion and Belief Systems: Civilization often gives rise to complex belief systems and religions. These systems provide moral and ethical guidance, shape cultural practices, and often influence political structures.

8. Trade and Interaction: Civilizations engage in trade and interaction with neighboring societies. This exchange of goods, ideas, and technologies fosters cultural diffusion and can lead to cultural enrichment.

9. Infrastructure and Architecture: Civilizations build impressive infrastructure and architectural marvels. This includes roads, bridges, temples, palaces, and other monumental structures that reflect their engineering and artistic prowess.

10. Political Institutions: Civilizations establish political institutions to govern their territories. These institutions can take various forms, from monarchies and democracies to empires and republics, depending on the civilization's historical and cultural context.

11. Education and Knowledge: Civilizations value education and the accumulation of knowledge. They often have centers of learning, such as universities and libraries, where scholars pursue research and intellectual growth.

12. Longevity and Legacy: Civilizations endure over long periods, leaving a lasting legacy. Their contributions to human progress, in terms of science, philosophy, culture, and governance, continue to influence subsequent generations.
It's important to note that civilizations can vary significantly in terms of their specific characteristics and historical trajectories. Not all civilizations exhibit all of the mentioned features, and the dynamics within each civilization can be intricate and unique.

Throughout history, various civilizations have risen and fallen, leaving indelible marks on human history. Examples of renowned civilizations include the ancient Egyptian, Mesopotamian, Indus Valley, Greek, Roman, Chinese, and Islamic civilizations, among many others. Civilization represents the zenith of human cultural and societal development, characterized by social organization, technological advancement, cultural achievements, urbanization, and more. It is a testament to humanity's capacity for progress, adaptation, and the pursuit of knowledge and excellence. Civilization has been defined by numerous authors, historians, and scholars over the years. Here are some notable definitions:

1. Will Durant: The historian Will Durant defined civilization as "social order promoting cultural creation." He emphasized the role of culture and creativity in shaping civilizations.

2. Lewis Mumford: Mumford, a prominent sociologist, saw civilization as "the art of living together in cities." He highlighted the significance of urbanization in the development of civilizations.

3. Arnold J. Toynbee: Toynbee, a renowned historian, defined civilization as "a society in a state of vigorous organic growth, tending to expand its boundaries and to create a lasting new culture." He focused on the dynamic nature of civilizations.

4. Samuel P. Huntington: In his book "The Clash of Civilizations and the Remaking of World Order," Huntington defined civilization as "the highest cultural grouping of people and the broadest level of cultural identity people have short of that which distinguishes humans from other species." He explored the role of civilizations in contemporary geopolitics.

5. Oswald Spengler: Spengler, in his work "The Decline of the West," defined civilization as "a body of spiritual, intellectual, ethical and political traditions held in common by a people." He examined the rise and fall of civilizations throughout history.

6. Edward Said: Said, in his influential book "Orientalism," discussed how the West historically perceived the East as the "other" and defined civilization as "a late 19th-century European invention."

7. Fernand Braudel: Braudel, a historian known for his work on world history, viewed civilization as "a particular way of life, which takes its shape from economic and social structures and from the milieu in which they operate."
These definitions vary in their emphasis, ranging from cultural creativity and social order to geographic and historical contexts. Civilization remains a multifaceted and evolving concept, subject to interpretation and analysis by scholars from various disciplines. Civilization, as understood by these authors, is a multifaceted concept encompassing cultural, social, and historical dimensions. It's the product of human ingenuity and collective effort, giving rise to organized societies, urban centers, and cultural expressions. Will Durant's emphasis on cultural creation underscores the role of art, literature, and intellectual achievements in defining a civilization's essence. Lewis Mumford's urban-centric perspective highlights the pivotal role of cities as centers of innovation and interaction. Arnold J. Toynbee's dynamic view acknowledges the growth, expansion, and cultural evolution that civilizations undergo. Samuel P. Huntington's focus on cultural identity connects civilization with contemporary global politics, while Oswald Spengler's historical analysis reveals patterns of rise and decline. Edward Said's exploration of Orientalism sheds light on the power dynamics and biases inherent in civilizational interpretations. Finally, Fernand Braudel's holistic approach integrates economic, social, and geographical factors in understanding civilization's unique way of life. These diverse definitions collectively underscore civilization's complex and evolving nature, shaped by history, culture, and human endeavor.

Difference between Culture and Civilization

Culture and civilization are two closely related concepts, often used interchangeably, but they have distinct meanings and characteristics. Understanding the differences between them can provide insight into the complexity of human societies.

1. **Definition and Scope:**

- **Culture:** Culture refers to the shared beliefs, values, customs, traditions, behaviors, and artifacts of a particular group of people or society. It encompasses the way people think, interact, and express themselves. Culture can be specific to a smaller community, subculture, or even an individual, and it encompasses various aspects of life, including language, art, religion, cuisine, and social norms.

- **Civilization:** Civilization is a broader concept that refers to the advanced stage of human social development characterized by complex social, political, economic, and technological systems. It involves organized societies, urbanization, and the presence of various institutions. While culture is a part of civilization, civilization also includes other elements like governance, infrastructure, and societal organization.

2. **Scale and Complexity**:

- **Culture:** Culture can exist at various scales, from small tribal communities to entire nations. It can be simple or complex, depending on the group's size and history. It often evolves slowly over time and can vary significantly from one group to another.

Civilization

Civilization typically refers to larger, more complex societies that have reached a certain level of development. It involves the organization of large populations, the establishment of cities, and the presence of intricate systems such as governments, legal codes, and advanced technologies. Civilizations are generally characterized by a higher degree of complexity than individual cultures.

3. **Societal Organization:**

- **Culture:** Culture does not necessarily require a highly organized societal structure. It can exist within small communities or even among individuals who share common beliefs and practices. Cultural elements can be passed down through generations informally.

- **Civilization:** Civilizations are marked by advanced societal organization. They have complex political structures, including governments and legal systems, which help regulate and manage the larger population. Cities are typically the centers of civilization, where economic, political, and cultural activities are concentrated.

4. **Technological Advancement:**

- **Culture:** Cultural practices can be associated with a wide range of technological advancements, from simple traditional tools to sophisticated art forms. However, the level of technological advancement can vary greatly among different cultures.

- **Civilization:** Civilizations are often associated with significant technological advancements. They tend to develop advanced agricultural practices, infrastructure like roads and buildings, and more sophisticated tools and technologies that contribute to their growth and expansion.

5. **Historical Perspective:**

- **Culture:** Culture can be timeless and enduring, passed down through generations with deep-rooted traditions. It can evolve slowly over time but may retain core elements that connect it to its historical origins.

- **Civilization:** Civilizations often have a historical trajectory, with identifiable periods of rise, peak, and decline. They leave behind a historical record of their achievements, and the study of civilizations often involves examining their historical development and legacy

6. **Urbanization**:

- **Culture:** Culture can exist in both urban and rural settings, and it is not inherently tied to urbanization. Cultural practices can be found in diverse environments.

- **Civilization:** Urbanization, the development of cities, is a characteristic feature of civilizations. Cities serve as hubs for economic, political, and cultural activities, and they are often a defining element of civilizations.

7. **Governance and Legal Systems**:

Culture:

Cultural practices may or may not be associated with formal governance structures and legal systems. In smaller cultural groups, informal norms and traditions may suffice for regulating behavior.

- **Civilization:** Civilizations have more complex governance structures, including formal governments and legal systems. These systems help manage larger populations and ensure order and stability within the society.

8. **Scale of Influence**:

- **Culture:** Culture can influence individuals, smaller groups, or specific regions. It often defines the identity and way of life of a particular group of people.

Civilizations have a broader influence and impact. They can shape the destinies of entire regions or even have a global influence, affecting politics, trade, and cultural exchange on a larger scale.

9. **Relationship between Culture and Civilization:**

- **Culture within Civilization:** Culture is an integral part of civilizations. Civilizations are composed of various cultural groups, each with its own set of beliefs, values, and traditions. These cultural elements contribute to the overall identity and character of the civilization.

- **Culture outside Civilization:** Culture is not limited to civilizations. It can exist in smaller groups and communities that may not meet the criteria for a full-fledged civilization. In fact, many cultural practices and traditions originate in smaller, non-civilized groups.

10. Adaptability and Change:

- **Culture:** Cultural practices can be highly adaptable and may change over time in response to internal and external influences. Cultures can be dynamic and flexible.

- **Civilization:** While civilizations can adapt and change, they often exhibit more resistance to rapid change due to their complex structures and institutions. Changes in civilizations often occur over longer periods.

Culture and civilization are distinct but interconnected concepts. Culture represents the beliefs, values, and practices of a specific group of people, while civilization refers to the broader, more complex societal structures that include organized governance, urbanization, and technological advancement. While culture can exist within and outside of civilizations, it is a vital component of the larger framework of civilization. Understanding these differences helps us appreciate the multifaceted nature of human societies and their development throughout history. In essence, culture and civilization are like concentric circles, with culture forming the core of a civilization. While culture encompasses the beliefs, traditions, and customs that define a group's identity, civilization extends beyond, including the complex systems and structures that emerge as societies grow. Culture is the soul, the deeply rooted identity, while civilization represents the body, the organized, often urban, societal structure. Recognizing these differences illuminates the intricate interplay between shared values and the broader mechanisms that shape human societies, enriching our understanding of the diverse tapestry of human existence.

Geographical and historical context of Culture and Civilization in India

The geographical and historical context of culture and civilization in India is a tapestry woven over millennia. India's rich and diverse cultural heritage has been shaped by its vast landscape, historical events, and a tapestry of peoples, religions, and traditions. This context is essential for understanding the depth and complexity of Indian culture and civilization.

Geographical Context:

India's geographical diversity has played a pivotal role in shaping its culture and civilization. The Indian subcontinent is geographically diverse, encompassing mountains, plains, deserts, forests, and a vast coastline. Key geographical features include:

1. The Himalayas: To the north, the towering Himalayan Mountain range acts as a natural barrier, influencing climate patterns and migration. These mountains are not only a geographical feature but also a spiritual and cultural symbol in Indian civilization, often associated with Hinduism and Buddhism.

2. The Indo-Gangetic Plain: This fertile region, stretching from the Indus River in the west to the Ganges River in the east, has been the cradle of Indian civilization. Its fertile soils have supported agriculture for thousands of years and have given rise to great empires and cities.

3. Western and Eastern Coasts: India's extensive coastline along the Arabian Sea and the Bay of Bengal has facilitated trade, cultural exchange, and maritime activities for centuries. Coastal regions have their unique cultural identities.

4. Thar Desert: The arid Thar Desert in the northwest has influenced the culture and lifestyles of the people living in this region.

5. Western and Eastern Ghats: These mountain ranges run parallel to the coasts and have influenced local climate, ecology, and culture.

6. Deccan Plateau: The vast Deccan Plateau in the central part of India has been a hub for various dynasties and empires throughout history.

7. Islands: India includes several islands in the Indian Ocean, such as the Andaman and Nicobar Islands, each with its unique cultural and ecological characteristics.

Historical Context:

India's history is marked by a succession of empires, kingdoms, and dynasties that have left their indelible marks on its culture and civilization. The historical context can be divided into several key periods:

1. Indus Valley Civilization (circa 3300–1300 BCE): India's earliest urban civilization, characterized by planned cities like Mohenjo-Daro and Harappa, showcased advanced urban planning and trade networks. While much of its writing remains undeciphered, it laid the foundation for many cultural practices in India.

2. Vedic Period (circa 1500–500 BCE): The arrival of the Indo-Aryans marked the Vedic period. The Vedas, ancient sacred texts, were composed during this time and introduced concepts central to Hinduism. The caste system, rituals, and early religious practices emerged during this era.

3. Maurya and Gupta Empires (circa 4th century BCE to 6th century CE): These empires witnessed remarkable advancements in science, mathematics, art, and governance. The Mauryan Emperor Ashoka embraced Buddhism, which left a lasting impact on Indian culture.

4. Medieval Period (circa 7th to 18th century CE): This era saw the rise and fall of various dynasties and empires, including the Delhi Sultanate and the Mughal Empire. It was a period of cultural fusion, marked by the spread of Islam, the flourishing of art and architecture, and the synthesis of Hindu and Islamic traditions.

5. British Colonial Rule (1757–1947 CE): The British East India Company's arrival in India led to colonial rule. The struggle for independence and the efforts of leaders like Mahatma Gandhi and Jawaharlal Nehru played a pivotal role in shaping modern India.

6. Post-Independence Era (1947–Present): India gained independence in 1947, leading to the formation of the Republic of India. This period has seen rapid modernization, urbanization, and economic development, alongside the preservation of cultural heritage and diversity.

Cultural and Civilizational Aspects:

1. Religions: India is the birthplace of major religions, including Hinduism, Buddhism, Jainism, and Sikhism. These religions have had a profound influence on Indian culture and civilization, shaping religious practices, rituals, and festivals.

2. Language Diversity: India is incredibly linguistically diverse, with over 1,600 languages spoken. This linguistic diversity has contributed to a rich tapestry of literature, art, and cultural traditions.

3. Cuisine: Indian cuisine is renowned worldwide for its diversity and flavors. Each region has its culinary specialties, influenced by geography, climate, and culture.

4. Art and Architecture: India boasts a remarkable legacy of art and architecture, from the intricately carved temples of Khajuraho to the majestic Taj Mahal. These structures reflect various historical periods and artistic styles.

5. Music and Dance: India's classical music and dance forms, such as Hindustani and Carnatic music and Bharatanatyam, have deep-rooted traditions and continue to thrive in contemporary society.

6. Literature: Indian literature includes ancient texts like the Vedas and epics like the Ramayana and Mahabharata, as well as modern literary giants like Rabindranath Tagore and R.K. Narayan.

7. Philosophy and Thought: India has a rich philosophical heritage, including schools of thought like Vedanta, Nyaya, and Sankhya, which have influenced not only Indian society but also global philosophical discourse.

8. Traditions and Rituals: India's cultural fabric is woven with diverse traditions and rituals, from the celebration of Diwali to the observance of Eid. These traditions vary by region and religion.

9. Clothing: Traditional Indian clothing, such as sarees, dhotis, and turbans, reflects the country's cultural diversity. Clothing styles often have historical and regional significance.

10. Yoga and Ayurveda: India is the birthplace of yoga and Ayurveda, ancient systems of physical and mental well-being that continue to be practiced worldwide.

11. Festivals: India celebrates a multitude of festivals throughout the year, each with its unique cultural and religious significance. Festivals like Holi, Eid, and Christmas are celebrated with great fervor.

12. Cultural Fusion: India's history of trade and conquest has led to cultural fusion. For example, the Mughal period saw the fusion of Persian and Indian architectural styles, while Indian cuisine incorporates influences from various regions.
The geographical and historical context of culture and civilization in India is a vast and intricate mosaic. India's diverse landscape, along with its complex historical journey, has given rise to a rich and multifaceted culture and civilization that continues to evolve and flourish in the modern era. Understanding this context is essential for appreciating the depth and diversity of India's cultural heritage.

- Geographical, chronological, and cultural scope of ancient India

The geographical, chronological, and cultural scope of ancient India is a tapestry that weaves together a vast and diverse landscape, a timeline stretching back millennia, and a rich cultural heritage. Exploring these dimensions provides insight into the depth and complexity of ancient Indian civilization.

Geographical Scope:

Ancient India encompassed a wide and varied geographical expanse, with distinct regions that played pivotal roles in shaping its history and culture:

1. The Indus Valley: The Indus Valley, located in what is now Pakistan, was home to one of the world's earliest urban civilizations, the Indus Valley Civilization (circa 3300–1300 BCE). Cities like Mohenjo-Daro and Harappa thrived along the banks of the Indus River, showcasing advanced urban planning and trade networks.

2. The Gangetic Plain: The fertile plains of the Ganges River in northern India have been the heartland of Indian civilization for millennia. It served as the backdrop for the emergence of Vedic culture, which laid the foundation for Hinduism.

3. The Deccan Plateau: The vast Deccan Plateau in central India was a region of great historical significance. It witnessed the rise and fall of various empires and dynasties, contributing to India's cultural mosaic.

4. The Western Ghats and the Malabar Coast: The lush Western Ghats and the Malabar Coast along the Arabian Sea have influenced local cultures, biodiversity, and trade for centuries.

5. The Eastern Coast: The eastern coastline along the Bay of Bengal was a hub for maritime activities, trade, and cultural exchange.

6. The Himalayas: The towering Himalayan Mountain range in the north served as a natural border and influence weather patterns, trade routes, and cultural interactions.

7. The Thar Desert: The arid Thar Desert in the northwest shaped the lifestyles and culture of the people living in this challenging environment.

8. Islands: India includes several islands, such as the Andaman and Nicobar Islands, each with its unique cultural and ecological characteristics.

Chronological Scope:

The ancient history of India spans a vast chronological range, divided into several key periods:

1. Indus Valley Civilization (circa 3300–1300 BCE): This was one of the earliest urban civilizations in the world, known for its sophisticated urban planning and trade networks. It predates most of the historical periods in India.

2. Vedic Period (circa 1500–500 BCE): The arrival of the Indo-Aryans marked the Vedic period. It saw the composition of the Vedas, ancient sacred texts that introduced concepts central to Hinduism.

3. Maurya and Gupta Empires (circa 4th century BCE to 6th century CE): These empires witnessed significant advancements in science, mathematics, art, and governance. The Mauryan Emperor Ashoka's embrace of Buddhism had a lasting impact on Indian culture.

4. Medieval Period (circa 7th to 18th century CE): This era saw the rise and fall of various dynasties and empires, including the Delhi Sultanate and the Mughal Empire. It was a period of cultural fusion, marked by the spread of Islam and the synthesis of Hindu and Islamic traditions.

5. British Colonial Rule (1757–1947 CE) : The British East India Company's arrival led to colonial rule. It also marked the beginning of modern Indian history and the struggle for independence, which culminated in 1947.

6. post-Independence Era (1947–Present): India gained independence in 1947, leading to the formation of the Republic of India. This period has seen rapid modernization, urbanization, and economic development, alongside the preservation of cultural heritage and diversity.

Cultural Scope: The cultural diversity of ancient India is a testament to its rich heritage and legacy. This diversity is reflected in various aspects of culture:

1. Religions: Ancient India gave birth to major religions, including Hinduism, Buddhism, Jainism, and Sikhism. These religions shaped religious practices, rituals, and festivals. Buddhism spread to various parts of Asia.

2. Language Diversity: India's linguistic diversity is remarkable, with over 1,600 languages spoken. This diversity has contributed to a rich tapestry of literature, art, and cultural traditions.

3. Cuisine: Indian cuisine is renowned for its diversity and flavors. Each region has its culinary specialties, influenced by geography, climate, and culture. Spices and ingredients vary widely across the subcontinent.

4. Art and Architecture: Ancient India boasts a remarkable legacy of art and architecture, from the intricately carved temples of Khajuraho to the majestic Taj Mahal. These structures reflect various historical periods and artistic styles.

5. Music and Dance: India's classical music and dance forms, such as Hindustani and Carnatic music and Bharatanatyam, have deep-rooted traditions and continue to thrive in contemporary society.

6. Literature: Ancient Indian literature includes texts like the Vedas, epics like the Ramayana and Mahabharata, and works of classical literature. The poetry of Kalidasa and philosophical treatises like the Arthashastra is celebrated examples.

7. Philosophy and Thought: India has a rich philosophical heritage, including schools of thought like Vedanta, Nyaya, and Sankhya, which have influenced not only Indian society but also global philosophical discourse.

8. Traditions and Rituals: Ancient India's cultural fabric is woven with diverse traditions and rituals, from the celebration of Diwali to the observance of Eid. These traditions vary by region and religion.

9. Clothing: Traditional Indian clothing, such as sarees, dhotis, and turbans, reflects the country's cultural diversity. Clothing styles often have historical and regional significance.

10. Yoga and Ayurveda: Ancient India is the birthplace of yoga and Ayurveda, ancient systems of physical and mental well-being that continue to be practiced worldwide.

11. Festivals: India celebrates a multitude of festivals throughout the year, each with its unique cultural and religious significance. Festivals like Holi, Eid, and Christmas are celebrated with great fervor.

12. Cultural Fusion: India's history of trade and conquest has led to cultural fusion. For example, the Mughal period saw the

fusion of Persian and Indian architectural styles, while Indian cuisine incorporates influences from various regions.
The geographical, chronological, and cultural scope of ancient India is a vast and intricate tapestry. The diverse landscapes, historical periods, and cultural expressions have contributed to India's unique identity and enduring cultural heritage. This scope provides a glimpse into the profound richness and complexity of India's ancient civilization.

- A brief overview of the major historical periods and empires in ancient India.

Ancient India's history is marked by a succession of major historical periods and empires, each leaving its distinct imprint on the subcontinent's culture, society, and heritage. Here is a brief overview of some of the significant historical periods and empires in ancient India:

1. Indus Valley Civilization (circa 3300–1300 BCE):- The Indus Valley Civilization was one of the world's earliest urban civilizations, located in what is now Pakistan and northwest India.
- Known for advanced urban planning, a system of writing, and trade networks.
- Key cities included Mohenjo-Daro and Harappa.
- Economy based on agriculture and trade.
- Mysterious decline and abandonment, possibly due to environmental factors.

2. Vedic Period (circa 1500–500 BCE): - Characterized by the arrival of Indo-Aryans into the Indian subcontinent.
- Vedas, the oldest sacred texts of Hinduism, composed during this time.
- Emergence of caste system and rituals.

- Rigveda is one of the earliest Vedic texts.

3. Maurya Empire (circa 322–185 BCE): - Founded by Chandragupta Maurya, who unified much of the Indian subcontinent.

- Under Ashoka, the empire expanded further and embraced Buddhism.
- First centralized and extensive political empire in ancient India.
- Flourishing trade and administration.

4. Gupta Empire (circa 4th to 6th century CE): - The Gupta Empire is often considered the Golden Age of ancient India.

- Flourishing of art, culture, and scholarship.
- Decimal numeral system and concept of zero developed.
- Fa-Hien and Xuanzang, Chinese travelers, visited during this period.
- Extensive maritime trade.

5. Post-Gupta Period (circa 6th to 8th century CE): - Following the decline of the Gupta Empire, the Indian subcontinent witnessed the rise of numerous regional kingdoms.

- Art and literature continued to thrive.
- Emergence of classical Indian dance and poetry.

6. Chola Dynasty (circa 9th to 13th century CE): - Based in southern India, the Chola Dynasty was known for its naval power and maritime trade.

- The dynasty expanded its influence overseas, including Southeast Asia.
- Great temple construction, including the Brihadeeswarar Temple.

7. Delhi Sultanate (circa 13th to 16th century CE): - A series of Muslim dynasties ruled northern India, beginning with the

Ghurids and the Slave Dynasty.

- Sultanate rulers introduced Persian and Islamic influences.
- The Delhi Sultanate laid the foundation for the Mughal Empire.

8. Vijayanagara Empire (circa 14th to 17th century CE):- A powerful empire in the Deccan region of southern India.

- Known for its grand architecture, including the Hampi ruins.
- Flourishing trade and culture.
- Ruled by various dynasties, including the Sangama and Saluva.

9. Mughal Empire (circa 16th to 19th century CE):- Founded by Babur in 1526, the Mughal Empire became one of the most significant empires in Indian history.

- Emperors like Akbar, Jahangir, and Shah Jahan presided over a period of cultural and architectural splendor.
- Mughal art, including the Taj Mahal, remains iconic.
- Religious tolerance and syncretism under Akbar's rule.
- Decline in the later years, with British colonial influence growing.

10. Maratha Empire (circa 17th to 19th century CE):- Based in western India, the Marathas emerged as a dominant power after the decline of the Mughal Empire.

- Chhatrapati Shivaji is a celebrated Maratha ruler known for his administration and naval prowess.
- The empire played a significant role in resisting British colonial expansion.

11. Sikh Empire (circa 18th to 19th century CE): - The Sikh Empire, founded by Maharaja Ranjit Singh, was centered in the Punjab region of northern India.

- Sikhs introduced religious and administrative reforms.
- The empire resisted British expansion but eventually

succumbed to British rule.

12. British Colonial Rule (1757–1947 CE):- The British East India Company's arrival marked the beginning of British colonial rule in India.

- India became a British colony, with profound political, social, and economic changes.
- The struggle for independence, led by figures like Mahatma Gandhi, resulted in India gaining independence in 1947.

These historical periods and empires provide a glimpse into the rich and varied history of ancient India. They showcase the evolution of political power, cultural achievements, religious movements, and the resilience of India's diverse societies over thousands of years. The legacy of these periods continues to influence modern India's cultural, political, and social landscape.

- **The significance of culture and Civilisation in understanding the past**

Culture and civilization are of paramount significance in understanding the past because they serve as lenses through which we can explore the complexities of human history. Here are several key reasons why culture and civilization are crucial in comprehending the past:

1. Contextual Understanding: Culture and civilization provide the context in which historical events and developments occurred. They offer insights into the values, beliefs, norms, and practices of the people of a particular time and place. This contextual understanding is essential for interpreting the motives and actions of historical actors.

2. Cultural Heritage: Culture and civilization preserve the collective heritage of societies. They encompass literature, art, architecture, music, and other forms of expression that not only reflect the past but also shape the identity of a community. Exploring this heritage allows us to appreciate the depth of human creativity and ingenuity throughout history.

3. Social Structures: Culture and civilization reveal the social structures and hierarchies that existed in the past. They help us understand issues related to class, gender, religion, and ethnicity, shedding light on the roles and statuses of different segments of society.

4. Cultural Exchange: Interactions between cultures and civilizations have been a driving force in human history. Trade, conquest, migration, and diplomacy have led to the exchange of ideas, technologies, and practices. Studying these interactions helps us trace the diffusion of knowledge and innovations across regions and time periods.

5. Evolution and Change: Culture and civilization evolve over time. By examining the changes and adaptations within a society's culture and civilization, historians can trace the evolution of societal norms, technologies, and institutions. This provides insights into the dynamics of historical change.

6. Conflict and Cooperation: Understanding the cultural and civilizational dimensions of historical conflicts and alliances is crucial. It helps us analyze the causes and consequences of wars, treaties, and diplomatic relations. Cultural factors often play a role in shaping the outcomes of these interactions.

7. Identity and Belonging: Culture and civilization contribute to individual and group identities. They influence how people perceive themselves and their place in the world. Historical analysis of cultural identities and affiliations helps us comprehend the motivations and loyalties of historical actors.

8. Legacy and Influence: The legacies of past cultures and civilizations endure in contemporary societies. Ideas, traditions, and institutions from the past continue to shape our present. By examining historical cultures and civilizations, we can trace the roots of modern ideologies, practices, and conflicts.

9. Comparative Analysis: Studying multiple cultures and civilizations allows for comparative analysis. This comparative approach helps historians identify patterns, similarities, and differences across time and place, leading to a deeper understanding of human history.

10. Interdisciplinary Insights: Culture and civilization are inherently interdisciplinary topics. Historians collaborate with scholars from fields such as anthropology, archaeology, sociology, and religious studies to gain holistic perspectives on the past. This interdisciplinary approach enriches historical research.

11. Preservation of Heritage: The study and preservation of cultural and civilizational heritage are essential for safeguarding the historical record. Museums, archives, and cultural institutions play a vital role in preserving artifacts, documents, and traditions that provide valuable insights into the past.

Culture and civilization are indispensable tools for historians and scholars to navigate the complexities of the past. They offer a multidimensional framework for understanding the social, economic, political, and intellectual dimensions of historical societies. By delving into culture and civilization, we gain a deeper appreciation of the diversity of human experiences and the intricate tapestry of our shared history.

- The significance of understanding ancient Indian culture in the context of development.

Understanding ancient Indian culture is of profound significance in the context of development, as it provides a foundation upon which modern India has evolved. This cultural understanding informs various aspects of development, including social, economic, political, and environmental dimensions. Here are key reasons why ancient Indian culture is significant for development:

1. Cultural Identity and Unity: - Ancient Indian culture forms the bedrock of India's cultural identity. It unites a diverse nation with numerous languages, religions, and traditions.

- This cultural identity fosters a sense of belonging and national pride, contributing to social cohesion and stability, which are essential for sustainable development.

2. Cultural Values and Social Development: - Ancient Indian culture is imbued with values such as compassion, tolerance, and non-violence, which are essential for fostering inclusive and harmonious societies.

- These values underpin social development efforts, including poverty alleviation, education, and healthcare, by promoting empathy and social responsibility.

3. Traditional Knowledge and Sustainable Practices:- Ancient Indian culture encompasses a wealth of traditional knowledge in fields like agriculture, medicine (Ayurveda), and architecture (Vastu Shastra).

- This knowledge can be harnessed to develop sustainable practices that address modern challenges, such as climate change and food security.

4. Cultural Heritage Tourism: - India's rich cultural heritage, including ancient temples, monuments, and traditions, attracts millions of tourists annually.

- Tourism contributes significantly to the country's economic development, generating income and employment opportunities.

5. Art and Craftsmanship: - Ancient Indian culture has a long history of artistic and craft traditions, including painting, sculpture, textiles, and jewelry.

- The preservation and promotion of these crafts contribute to economic development by creating livelihoods and promoting exports.

6. Philosophy and Well-being: - Ancient Indian philosophy, including yoga and meditation, promotes physical and mental well-being.

- Incorporating these practices into healthcare and education can lead to healthier, more productive populations, which are integral to development.

7. Cultural Diplomacy:- India's cultural heritage serves as a powerful tool for diplomacy and international relations.

- Cultural exchange programs and collaborations foster positive relationships and economic opportunities with other nations.

8. Social Inclusion and Empowerment: - Ancient Indian culture includes stories and teachings that emphasize social justice and the rights of marginalized groups.

- Drawing upon these cultural narratives can promote social inclusion and empower disadvantaged communities.

9. Education and Innovation: - Ancient India had renowned centers of learning like Nalanda and Takshashila, where scholars from diverse backgrounds pursued knowledge.

- Revisiting these historical models can inspire educational innovations and research excellence, driving economic growth.

10. Language Preservation: - Ancient Indian culture encompasses a multitude of languages and scripts.

- Preserving and promoting linguistic diversity can enhance communication and contribute to cultural richness, benefiting development efforts.

11. Governance and Ethics: - Ancient Indian texts, such as the Arthashastra, offer insights into governance, ethics, and administration.

- Ethical governance principles can foster transparency and accountability, crucial for effective development initiatives.

12. Cultural Entrepreneurship: - The unique cultural offerings of India, including music, dance, and festivals, provide opportunities for cultural entrepreneurship.

- This sector can generate economic growth and promote cultural exchange.

13. Environmental Stewardship: - Ancient Indian culture includes a reverence for nature and the environment.

- These cultural values can inform sustainable development practices and environmental conservation efforts.

14. Conflict Resolution: - Ancient Indian culture has a history of non-violent conflict resolution and dialogue.

- These principles can guide peacebuilding efforts, reducing conflicts that hinder development.

15. Cultural Resilience: - Understanding ancient Indian culture's resilience over millennia can inspire adaptability and innovation in the face of modern challenges.

- Cultural resilience is a valuable asset for addressing development-related crises.

16. Moral and Ethical Development: - Ancient Indian culture promotes moral and ethical development, emphasizing virtues like honesty, integrity, and humility.

- A society grounded in these values is more likely to achieve sustainable development goals.

Understanding ancient Indian culture is not merely an exercise in historical exploration; it is a critical asset for contemporary development. It provides a roadmap for harnessing traditional wisdom, cultural richness, and ethical principles to address the multifaceted challenges of the modern world. By integrating cultural insights into development strategies, India can promote inclusive, sustainable, and culturally rooted progress, ensuring a brighter future for its diverse population.

- **Key sources and methods used to study ancient Indian culture**

Studying ancient Indian culture involves a multidisciplinary approach, drawing from a wide range of sources and methods. These sources and methods provide valuable insights into the diverse aspects of India's rich cultural heritage. Here are key sources and methods used in the study of ancient Indian culture:

Sources:

1. Textual Sources:

- Ancient Indian texts, including religious scriptures like the Vedas, Upanishads, and Puranas, provide insights into religious beliefs, rituals, and philosophy.

- Historical texts such as the Ramayana, Mahabharata, and Arthashastra offer information on history, literature, governance, and social customs.

- Literary works, poetry, and plays by renowned authors like Kalidasa and Bhasa provide cultural and literary perspectives.

- Sanskrit classics like the Manusmriti and the works of scholars like Patanjali offer legal, ethical, and philosophical insights.

2. Inscriptions:

- Epigraphical inscriptions found on stone, metal, and other materials offer valuable historical and cultural information.

- They include inscriptions on temple walls, pillars, and coins, providing details about rulers, dynasties, and religious contributions.

3. Archaeological Discoveries:

- Archaeological excavations unearth artifacts, structures, and settlements that shed light on ancient lifestyles, technology, and trade.

- Iconic archaeological sites like the Indus Valley Civilization cities and Buddhist stupas have provided significant insights.

4. Art and Iconography:

- Ancient Indian art, including sculpture, painting, and iconography, offers visual representations of cultural and religious practices.

- Temples and cave complexes display intricate carvings and frescoes reflecting religious narratives and artistic styles.

5. Numismatics:

- Ancient Indian coins provide information about economic systems, trade routes, and political leadership.

- Coin inscriptions often include rulers' names and titles.

6. Manuscripts:

- Ancient manuscripts, written on materials like palm leaves and birch bark, contain literary, scientific, and philosophical texts.

- Preservation and translation of manuscripts contribute to the study of ancient Indian knowledge systems.

7. Ethnographic Studies:

- Ethnographic research among contemporary Indian communities provides insights into traditional customs, rituals, and oral traditions that have been passed down through generations.

8. Historical Travelogues:

- Travel accounts by ancient travelers like Fa-Hien, Xuanzang, and Megasthenes offer valuable observations of Indian society, culture, and governance during their respective eras.

Methods:

1. Linguistic Analysis:

- Linguistic studies involve the analysis of ancient Indian languages, scripts, and linguistic evolution.

- Comparative linguistics help trace the historical development of languages like Sanskrit, Prakrits, and Dravidian languages.

2. Historical Research:

- Historical research relies on the critical analysis of ancient texts, inscriptions, and archaeological findings to reconstruct historical timelines and events.

- Researchers often employ source criticism and cross-referencing to validate historical data.

3. Philological Analysis:

- Philology involves the study of ancient texts, their languages, and textual variations.

- Textual criticism helps determine the authenticity of manuscripts and identify changes over time.

4. Iconographic and Artistic Analysis:

- Scholars analyze ancient art and iconography to decipher religious and cultural symbolism.

- Stylistic analysis helps identify regional and chronological variations in artistic representations.

5. Ethnographic Fieldwork:

- Ethnographic methods involve fieldwork, participant observation, and interviews with contemporary communities practicing ancient traditions.

- Researchers document rituals, customs, and folklore that have survived through generations.

6. Scientific Dating Techniques:

- Radiocarbon dating, thermoluminescence, and other scientific methods help determine the age of archaeological artifacts and remains.

7. Digital Humanities:

- Modern technologies, such as digital databases and GIS (Geographic Information Systems), aid in cataloging, analyzing, and visualizing archaeological and historical data.

8. Interdisciplinary Approaches:

- Researchers often collaborate across disciplines, combining historical, archaeological, linguistic, and scientific methods to gain comprehensive insights into ancient Indian culture.

9. Comparative Studies:

- Comparative analysis involves comparing ancient Indian culture with other cultures, both within the Indian subcontinent and globally, to identify similarities, influences, and unique features.

10. Museum and Exhibition Curations:

- Museums and exhibitions play a crucial role in presenting ancient Indian culture to the public. Curators use artifacts, visuals, and interactive displays to convey historical and cultural narratives.

11. Translation and Interpretation:

- Scholars translate ancient texts into contemporary languages and provide interpretations to make them accessible to a wider audience.

The study of ancient Indian culture is a multidimensional endeavor that relies on a diverse array of sources and methodologies. By combining historical research, linguistic analysis, archaeological discoveries, and ethnographic studies, scholars and researchers can piece together a comprehensive understanding of India's rich cultural heritage and its significance in shaping both the past and present. The study of ancient Indian culture relies on diverse sources, including texts, inscriptions, art, and archaeology. Linguistic and historical research, along with interdisciplinary methods, help unravel the intricacies of India's cultural tapestry. Ethnographic fieldwork preserves living traditions, while scientific dating techniques provide chronological context. This holistic approach sheds light on India's profound cultural heritage, encompassing philosophy, art, language, and traditions, contributing to a deeper appreciation of its past and its relevance in contemporary society.

- The relevance of studying ancient cultures in today's globalized world

Studying ancient cultures remains highly relevant in today's globalized world for several compelling reasons:

1. Cultural Understanding:

Understanding ancient cultures fosters empathy and respect for diverse perspectives, crucial for navigating a multicultural and interconnected world.

2. Preservation of Heritage:

Ancient cultures hold invaluable historical, artistic, and intellectual legacies that enrich humanity's collective heritage.

3. Identity and Roots:

For individuals and communities, knowledge of ancient cultural roots strengthens their sense of identity and provides a foundation for personal and group pride.

4. Cultural Diplomacy:

Cultural exchanges and diplomacy based on shared cultural elements promote international cooperation and positive relations.

5. Innovation and Inspiration:

Ancient cultures inspire creativity and innovation by offering alternative viewpoints, artistic forms, and problem-solving approaches.

6. Historical Lessons:

Examining past cultures provides valuable lessons about successes and mistakes, informing modern decision-making and policy.

7. Social Harmony:

Learning from ancient cultures' approaches to social harmony and conflict resolution contributes to peace and social cohesion.

8. Sustainability:

Ancient cultures often practiced sustainable living, offering insights for addressing contemporary environmental challenges.

9. Resilience and Adaptation:

Studying ancient cultures' ability to adapt to changing circumstances inspires resilience in today's rapidly changing world.

10. Cultural Tourism:

Ancient cultural sites attract tourists, bolstering local economies and promoting cultural exchange.

In essence, ancient cultures offer profound wisdom and perspectives that remain indispensable in navigating the complexities of our globalized society. Studying ancient cultures in today's globalized world is not just a matter of historical curiosity; it has profound relevance and significance that extends to various aspects of modern life. Here, we find deeper into the multifaceted relevance of understanding ancient cultures in our contemporary, interconnected world.

1. Cultural Diversity and Tolerance:

- In our globalized society, people from diverse backgrounds interact daily. Understanding ancient cultures fosters tolerance and respect for different beliefs, practices, and worldviews, promoting social harmony and reducing prejudices.

2. Cross-Cultural Communication:

- Effective cross-cultural communication is vital in the globalized workforce. Knowledge of ancient cultures aids in navigating cultural nuances, enhancing collaboration, and fostering mutual understanding in international business and diplomacy.

3. Cultural Heritage Preservation:

- Ancient cultures are repositories of unique traditions, languages, art forms, and architectural marvels. Preserving this heritage is essential not only for cultural identity but also for tourism, which contributes significantly to many economies worldwide.

4. Identity and Belonging:

- In a world where individuals often have multiple cultural affiliations, understanding one's own ancient cultural roots provides a sense of belonging and identity. This self-awareness contributes to personal well-being and strengthens cultural bonds.

5. Conflict Resolution and Peacebuilding:

- Ancient cultures often contain wisdom on conflict resolution and peaceful coexistence. Lessons from history can inform modern strategies for mitigating conflicts, reducing violence, and promoting international peace.

6. Innovation and Creativity:

- Ancient cultures' unique perspectives and creative expressions inspire innovation in various fields, including art, design, literature, and technology. A diverse range of cultural influences fuels creativity and fosters fresh ideas.

7. Environmental Sustainability:

- Many ancient cultures had sustainable lifestyles closely connected to nature. Their practices, such as agriculture, resource management, and eco-friendly building techniques, offer valuable insights for addressing contemporary environmental challenges and achieving sustainability goals.

8. Ethical Frameworks:

- Ancient cultures often provided ethical frameworks and moral guidelines. These can be applied to modern ethical dilemmas, contributing to ethical decision-making in areas like business, politics, and technology.

9. Historical Context for Policy:

- Understanding the historical contexts of ancient cultures helps policymakers make informed decisions by drawing lessons from past successes and failures. This historical perspective can inform policies related to governance, social justice, and economic development.

10. Cultural Diplomacy:

- Ancient cultures serve as powerful tools for cultural diplomacy and soft power. Sharing cultural heritage and engaging in cultural exchanges enhances international relations and fosters goodwill between nations.

11. Adaptation and Resilience:

- Many ancient cultures demonstrated adaptability and resilience in the face of adversity. Their stories of survival and transformation inspire individuals and communities to navigate modern challenges with resilience and adaptability.

12. Tourism and Economic Benefits:

- Ancient cultural sites and festivals attract tourists, generating economic revenue and employment opportunities for local communities. This tourism also promotes cultural exchange and international understanding.

13. Inspiration for Education:

- Ancient cultures offer rich educational material that can inspire curiosity and lifelong learning. Incorporating these cultural elements into education enhances critical thinking and cultural awareness among students.

14. Cultural Hybridity:

- In a world marked by cultural hybridity, ancient cultural elements influence contemporary identities and artistic expressions. Understanding these origins enriches our appreciation of the modern cultural landscape.

15. Preservation of Language and Traditions:

- Many ancient languages and traditions are endangered. Studying and documenting them is essential for preserving linguistic and cultural diversity, which are valuable resources for global society.

16. Holistic Worldview:

- Ancient cultures often held holistic worldviews that integrated nature, spirituality, and human existence. This perspective can inform holistic approaches to modern challenges, including mental health and well-being.

The relevance of studying ancient cultures in today's globalized world is multifaceted and far-reaching. It extends beyond the realms of history and archaeology, shaping how we interact, innovate, communicate, and address contemporary challenges. Ancient cultures provide a reservoir of wisdom, diversity, and inspiration that enriches our global society, promotes tolerance, and contributes to a more interconnected and culturally enriched world. In a world marked by globalization, the significance of studying ancient cultures cannot be overstated. These cultures offer a treasure trove of knowledge, wisdom, and inspiration that inform our present and guide our future. They teach us the value of diversity, tolerance, and adaptability, crucial in our interconnected world. By understanding the cultural heritage of the past, we not only preserve our shared human history but also unlock insights that enrich fields from diplomacy to sustainability, from creativity to conflict resolution. Ancient cultures are not relics of the past; they are living sources of vitality that shape our modern world in profound and lasting ways.

Chapter 2

Vedic and Indus Valley Civilization

The Vedic and Indus Valley Civilizations are two significant ancient civilizations in the Indian subcontinent. The Indus Valley Civilization, flourishing around 3300–1300 BCE, featured advanced urban planning, a script yet to be fully deciphered, and trade networks. In contrast, the Vedic Period (circa 1500–500 BCE) marked the arrival of Indo-Aryans, known for their religious texts, the Vedas. These cultures coexisted but had distinct characteristics. The Vedic culture laid the foundation for Hinduism, while the Indus Valley Civilization's legacy remains a testament to early urban achievements. Together, they form the rich tapestry of India's ancient past.

The Vedic and Indus Valley Civilizations, though separate in time and geography, hold significant places in the history of ancient India.

The Indus Valley Civilization, dating back to around 3300–1300 BCE, is known for its impressive urban centers like Mohenjo-Daro and Harappa. It displayed remarkable urban planning, with well-organized streets and drainage systems. The Indus script, found on seals, remains undeciphered, leaving a mystery about their written language. This civilization thrived on agriculture, trade, and craftsmanship, leaving behind evidence of intricate pottery and jewelry.

The Vedic Period, on the other hand, began around 1500 BCE with the arrival of the Indo-Aryans into the Indian subcontinent. This era is marked by the composition of the Vedas, a collection of ancient religious texts that laid the foundations of Hinduism. The Vedic society was organized into varnas, the precursor of the caste system, and revolved around rituals and sacrificial ceremonies.

While these civilizations had different cultural and religious elements, they are part of India's historical continuum. Some scholars suggest a degree of interaction between the two, as Vedic texts mention the "Sarasvati River," possibly a reference to the ancient Ghaggar-Hakra river in the Indus Valley. This highlights the complexity and interplay of cultures in ancient India, contributing to the diverse tapestry of the subcontinent's heritage.

Both civilizations have left an enduring legacy in India's cultural, religious, and historical landscape. The Vedic traditions laid the philosophical groundwork for Hinduism, Buddhism, and Jainism, while the Indus Valley Civilization showcased early urban achievements and technological advancements. Understanding these civilizations offers a glimpse into India's multifaceted past, contributing to a richer appreciation of its cultural and historical heritage.

- The Rigvedic society and its religious practices

The Rigvedic society, which flourished during the Vedic period (circa 1500–500 BCE), is the earliest period of ancient Indian history for which we have significant textual records, primarily in the form of the Rigveda, one of the oldest religious texts in the world. Rigveda is composed of hymns, prayers, and chants dedicated to various deities, providing insights into the society's religious practices, beliefs, and way of life.

Social Structure:

- The Rigvedic society was organized into tribes and clans known as "jana" and "vish," respectively.

- These tribes were led by chiefs or "rajas" who held both political and religious authority.

- The society was primarily agrarian, with cattle rearing and agriculture as central economic activities.

- The "varna" system, which later evolved into the caste system, was in its early stages. Society was divided into four primary groups: Brahmins (priests and scholars), Kshatriyas (warriors and rulers), Vaishyas (farmers and merchants), and Shudras (laborers and servants).

Religious Beliefs and Deities:

- Rigvedic religion was polytheistic, with reverence for various deities associated with natural forces and cosmic elements.

- The most prominent deity in the Rigveda is Indra, the god of thunder and rain, celebrated for his strength and prowess in battles.

- Agni, the god of fire, held a central role as the intermediary between humans and the gods. Fire rituals ("yajna") were integral to Rigvedic religious practices.

- Varuna, associated with cosmic order and moral righteousness, played a role in upholding cosmic laws and maintaining order.

- Other deities included Ushas (the dawn), Mitra (associated with contracts and friendship), and Rudra (the precursor of Lord Shiva).

- The concept of "Devas" and "Asuras" was prevalent, representing benevolent and malevolent cosmic forces, respectively.

Religious Practices:

- Rituals and sacrifices formed the core of Rigvedic religious practices.

- "Yajnas" or fire sacrifices were central to worship. They involved offerings of clarified butter ("ghee"), grains, and soma (an intoxicating plant) into the sacred fire.

- The "hotri" priests recited hymns, invoking various deities, while the "agnihotri" priest managed the ritual fire.

- "Soma" was considered a divine elixir that facilitated communication with the gods when consumed during rituals.

- Animal sacrifices, including horses, cattle, and goats, were offered to appease deities and seek their blessings.

- "Sacrifices" were not merely material offerings but also symbolic acts with spiritual significance.

- The Rigveda contains numerous hymns dedicated to specific deities, recounting their attributes and roles in the cosmic order.

- Chants and hymns were recited during rituals, praising the gods and seeking their favor.

- The "Soma Mandala" is a dedicated section of the Rigveda containing hymns devoted to Soma, the sacred plant.

Priesthood and Ritual Specialists:

- The priesthood played a central role in Rigvedic society. Brahmin priests were responsible for conducting rituals and ensuring the correct recitation of hymns.

-

They were revered for their knowledge of rituals and their ability to communicate with the divine.

- The chief priest, known as the "hotar," was assisted by various other priests and ritual specialists.

- Priests underwent rigorous training and were expected to maintain ritual purity.

- The "Rigveda" itself served as both a religious and educational text, containing hymns and knowledge about rituals.

Religious Concepts:

- Rigvedic religion emphasized the concept of "Rita," which represented the cosmic order and moral law governing the universe.

- The idea of "Dharma" was also present, signifying righteousness, duty, and ethical conduct.

- The concept of "Karma" (the consequences of one's actions) had its roots in these early religious beliefs.

- Rigvedic hymns reflected a deep connection with nature and the elements. The sun, moon, earth, and various natural phenomena were revered as divine manifestations.

Afterlife and Ancestors:

- Beliefs about the afterlife were less developed in the Rigvedic period compared to later Vedic periods.

- Ancestor worship was prominent, with offerings made to deceased ancestors to ensure their well-being in the afterlife.

- The "Pitris" or ancestors were believed to reside in the realm of the departed ("Pitri-loka").

The Rigvedic society's religious practices and beliefs were deeply rooted in the reverence for natural forces, cosmic order, and a pantheon of deities. Rituals and sacrifices were central to their religious life, conducted by a specialized priesthood. The concepts of "Rita," "Dharma," and "Karma" laid the foundation for moral and ethical principles that continue to influence Hindu philosophy and spirituality today. The Rigveda serves not only as a historical record of these early beliefs but also as a source of profound spiritual and philosophical insights that continue to shape Indian culture and thought.

- Social structure, roles, and responsibilities

The social structure and roles in Rigvedic society were delineated by a hierarchical system based on varnas (classes) and jatis (castes). This complex social order was central to the functioning of the society and influenced roles, responsibilities, and interactions among its members.

1. Varnas (Classes):

a. Brahmins (Priests and Scholars):

- **Roles and Responsibilities:** Brahmins were the highest varna and held the esteemed role of priests and scholars. They were responsible for conducting religious rituals and maintaining knowledge related to religious texts, including the Rigveda. They served as intermediaries between the human world and the divine.

- **Duties:** Conducting yajnas (sacrificial rituals), reciting sacred hymns, teaching, and performing rituals for the welfare of the community.

- **Privileges:** Enjoyed respect and reverence for their knowledge and spiritual authority.

b. Kshatriyas (Warriors and Rulers):

- **Roles and Responsibilities:** Kshatriyas held the second-highest position and were the rulers and warriors of the society. They were responsible for protecting the kingdom and maintaining law and order.

- **Duties:** Leading armies, defending the territory, ensuring justice, and upholding dharma (moral and ethical duties).

- **Privileges:** Held political power and authority.

c. Vaishyas (Farmers and Merchants):

- **Roles and Responsibilities:** Vaishyas were the third varna, engaged in agricultural and trade activities. They were responsible for the economic well-being of the society.

- **Duties:** Farming, trade, and commerce, contributing to economic prosperity, and supporting the state through taxation.

- **Privileges:** Enjoyed economic stability and the ability to accumulate wealth.

d. Shudras (Laborers and Servants):

- **Roles and Responsibilities:** Shudras occupied the lowest rung of the varna system. They were manual laborers and servants who provided essential services to the society.

- **Duties:** Serving the higher varnas, performing tasks deemed impure, and assisting in various capacities.

- **Privileges:** Had limited social and economic rights, but their labor was indispensable.

2. Jatis (Castes):

- Below the varnas, society was further divided into numerous jatis or castes, often associated with specific professions or occupations. The jati system added a layer of complexity to the social structure.

- Jatis included groups like blacksmiths, weavers, potters, and more, each with its unique roles and responsibilities.

- Jatis operated within the broader varna framework, with individuals belonging to specific jatis inheriting their occupations and social status.

Roles and Responsibilities Within the Family:

1. The Father (Pati/Pitri):

- **Roles and Responsibilities:** The father was the head of the family, responsible for providing for the family's material needs and protection. He played a central role in religious rituals and ceremonies.

- **Duties:** Ensuring the family's economic well-being, conducting rituals, imparting knowledge to the children, and maintaining discipline.

- **Privileges:** Held authority and decision-making power within the family.

2. The Mother (Mata/Matri):

- **Roles and Responsibilities:** The mother was responsible for managing the household, taking care of the children, and maintaining the family's domestic affairs.

- **Duties:** Cooking, cleaning, child-rearing, preserving family traditions, and supporting the husband in his responsibilities.

- **Privileges:** Held a respected position as the nurturer and caregiver of the family.

3. The Children (Putra/Putra and Putri/Putri):

- **Roles and Responsibilities:** Children were expected to obey their parents, learn from their elders, and prepare for their future roles within the society.

- **Duties:** Respect for parents, acquiring knowledge, and preparing for adulthood, including inheriting their family's profession and responsibilities.

- **Privileges:** Depended on their family's status and resources, with those in higher varnas having more opportunities.

4. Elders and Ancestors (Pitri):

- **Roles and Responsibilities:** Elders and ancestors held a revered position in the family. They were the custodians of family traditions and wisdom.

- **Duties:** Passing down knowledge, guiding family decisions, and ensuring the continuity of ancestral practices.

- **Privileges:** Commanded respect and were consulted for their wisdom and experience.

5. Siblings and Extended Family:

- **Roles and Responsibilities:** Siblings and extended family members provided emotional support and contributed to the family's well-being.

- **Duties:** Offering help during times of need, participating in family rituals, and maintaining close bonds.

- **Privileges:** Shared in the familial resources and support network.

Roles and Responsibilities in the Community:

1. Village Head/Chieftain:

- **Roles and Responsibilities:** The village head or chieftain was responsible for the administration and protection of the village or clan.

- **Duties:** Maintaining law and order, settling disputes, and representing the village in external matters.

- **Privileges:** Held authority and prestige in the community.

2. Religious Leaders and Priests:

- **Roles and Responsibilities:** Religious leaders and priests were responsible for conducting religious rituals, ceremonies, and sacrifices.

- **Duties:** Performing religious duties, maintaining temples and shrines, and imparting religious knowledge.

- **Privileges:** Enjoyed respect and reverence for their spiritual roles.

3. Craftsmen and Artisans:

- **Roles and Responsibilities:** Craftsmen and artisans were responsible for producing goods and crafts essential for daily life.

- **Duties:** Mastering their craft, producing quality products, and contributing to the local economy.

- **Privileges:** Valued for their skills and contributions.

4. Teachers and Scholars:

- **Roles and Responsibilities:** Teachers and scholars played a pivotal role in education and the transmission of knowledge.
- **Duties:** Imparting education, preserving cultural and intellectual traditions, and fostering intellectual growth.

- **Privileges:** Held in high regard for their role in shaping the minds of the next generation.

5. Laborers and Servants:

- **Roles and Responsibilities:** Laborers and servants performed various manual tasks essential for the functioning of society.

- **Duties:** Undertaking labor-intensive work, serving higher varnas, and contributing to the overall economy.

- **Privileges:** Had limited social and economic rights but played vital roles.

The Rigvedic society's social structure was hierarchically organized, with varnas and jatis defining roles and responsibilities. This complex system shaped individuals' positions within the family and community, influencing their duties and privileges based on their varna and jati affiliations. While it provided a framework for social order, it also posed challenges related to social mobility and discrimination, which would evolve and change in later periods of Indian history. The social structure and roles in Rigvedic society were highly stratified, with varnas and jatis determining individuals' positions and responsibilities. Brahmins were revered as priests and scholars, while Kshatriyas led as rulers and warriors. Vaishyas engaged in economic activities, and Shudras fulfilled essential labor roles. Within families, fathers provided for the household, mothers managed domestic affairs, and children learned their future roles. Elders and ancestors held revered positions. In the community, chieftains, religious leaders, craftsmen, teachers, and laborers all had distinct roles. This intricate system, while providing order, also led to inequalities, influencing the course of social development in ancient India.

The Rigvedic society's hierarchical structure, based on varnas and jatis, defined roles and responsibilities. Brahmins served as priests, Kshatriyas as rulers, Vaishyas as traders, and Shudras as laborers. Families operated with fathers as providers and mothers as caretakers. Elders preserved tradition, and children prepared for their societal roles. In the community, chieftains governed, religious leaders conducted rituals, and craftsmen, scholars, and laborers contributed to the community's well-being. This complex system maintained social order but also presented challenges of inequality, shaping the course of ancient Indian society and influencing its future development.

- Literature and philosophy of the Vedas

The Vedas, comprising the oldest sacred texts of Hinduism, hold a profound place in Indian literature and philosophy. These ancient scriptures are divided into four collections: the Rigveda, Yajurveda, Samaveda, and Atharvaveda. They encompass hymns, mantras, rituals, and philosophical insights that have shaped the spiritual and intellectual landscape of India for millennia.

1. Rigveda:

The Rigveda, the earliest Veda, consists of hymns dedicated to various deities and natural forces. It serves as the foundation for Vedic literature and philosophy.

a. Literature:

- The Rigveda contains over 1,000 hymns (suktas) composed in a poetic and metrical form.

- These hymns are primarily addressed to deities like Agni (fire), Indra (thunder and rain god), Varuna (cosmic order), and Ushas (the dawn).

- Themes encompass creation, cosmology, nature, rituals, and moral values.

b. Philosophy:

- The Rigveda introduces fundamental concepts like "Rita" (cosmic order), "Dharma" (duty/righteousness), and "Karma" (action and consequence).

- It emphasizes the interconnectedness of the universe and humanity's role within it.

- Philosophical hymns contemplate the nature of reality, the divine, and the human quest for knowledge.

2. Yajurveda:

The Yajurveda provides instructions and mantras for rituals and sacrifices. It is divided into two main versions: the Shukla Yajurveda and the Krishna Yajurveda.

a. Literature:

- The Yajurveda contains prose and verse portions designed for use by priests during rituals.

- It serves as a practical guide for performing various sacrificial ceremonies.

b. Philosophy:

- The Yajurveda focuses on the concept of "yajna" (sacrifice) as a means to establish harmony and order in the universe.

- It reinforces the idea of cosmic interconnectedness and the importance of rituals in maintaining cosmic balance.

3. Samaveda:

The Samaveda consists of chants and melodies that are sung during rituals. It emphasizes the musical aspect of the Vedic tradition.

a. Literature:

- The Samaveda is known for its poetic and musical qualities.

- It transforms Rigvedic verses into melodies for chanting during rituals.

b. Philosophy:

- While the Samaveda is primarily a liturgical text, it reinforces the significance of rituals and their role in aligning human actions with cosmic principles.

4. Atharvaveda:

The Atharvaveda contains hymns, spells, and incantations for a wide range of purposes, including healing, protection, and averting malevolent forces.

a. Literature:

- It includes both hymns for rituals and practical incantations for daily life.

- The Atharvaveda addresses various aspects of human existence, including health, well-being, and protection.

b. Philosophy:

- The Atharvaveda reflects a more practical and worldly approach to life, focusing on human concerns and well-being.

- It acknowledges the importance of addressing everyday challenges and seeking divine assistance.

Philosophical Themes in the Vedas:

1. Cosmic Order (Rita): The concept of "Rita" in the Vedas represents the cosmic order that governs the universe. It emphasizes the idea of a harmonious and structured world where everything has its place and purpose.

2. Dharma: The Vedas introduce the concept of "Dharma," which refers to one's duty, righteousness, and ethical conduct. It underscores the importance of individuals adhering to their prescribed roles and responsibilities in society.

3. Karma: The Vedas lay the foundation for the concept of "Karma," the idea that one's actions have consequences, both in this life and the next. It suggests that individuals are responsible for their actions and their effects.

4. Atman (Self): The Vedas contain hints of the idea of "Atman," the eternal and inner self, which becomes a central theme in later Vedic and philosophical literature.

5. Spiritual Quest: Philosophical hymns in the Vedas reflect on the nature of reality, the search for truth, and the human quest for knowledge and wisdom.

6. Interconnectedness: The Vedas emphasize the interconnectedness of all living beings and the cosmos, underscoring the idea that individuals are not isolated entities but part of a larger, cosmic whole.

The Vedas serve as the cornerstone of Indian literature and philosophy. They encompass a rich tapestry of hymns, rituals, and philosophical insights that explore the nature of the universe, the divine, and the human experience. These ancient texts have not only shaped the spiritual and philosophical traditions of India but also continue to inspire philosophical inquiry and spiritual exploration to this day.The Vedas, particularly the Rigveda, hold a special place in the development of philosophical thought in ancient India. They lay the foundational concepts and principles that would later be expanded upon in the Upanishads and form the basis of various schools of Indian philosophy.

Metaphysical Speculation:

While the Vedas primarily focus on rituals and hymns, they contain glimpses of profound metaphysical ideas. The hymns contemplate the nature of reality, the origin of the universe, and the relationship between the individual soul (Atman) and the ultimate reality (Brahman). These early metaphysical musings set the stage for deeper philosophical inquiries in later Vedic literature.

Ethical Foundations:

The Vedas introduce the concept of Dharma, emphasizing the importance of righteous conduct and moral duty. This ethical framework becomes central in later philosophical discussions about how individuals should live virtuous lives and fulfill their societal roles.

Theistic Foundations:

Although the Vedas feature polytheistic rituals, they also suggest a monotheistic undercurrent, hinting at the existence of a single, supreme reality (Brahman) behind the multitude of deities. This theistic aspect of the Vedas becomes a focal point for later Vedanta philosophy, which explores the nature of this ultimate reality.

Karma and Reincarnation:

The Vedas introduce the concept of Karma, the idea that one's actions have consequences. This notion is foundational in understanding the cycle of birth and rebirth (Samsara) and becomes a core concept in Indian philosophy, particularly in the context of schools like Vedanta, Buddhism, and Jainism. The Vedas emphasize the interconnectedness of all living beings and the cosmos, foreshadowing the interconnected worldview that later philosophies would elaborate on. This interconnectedness underscores the idea that every action has ripple effects in the cosmic order.

Symbiotic Relationship with Rituals:

The Vedas intertwine philosophy with rituals. The rituals and sacrifices prescribed in the Vedas are not merely external ceremonies but are seen as symbolic acts with spiritual significance. This synthesis of philosophy and practice underscores the belief that the pursuit of knowledge and spirituality should be integrated into daily life.

The Vedas represent not only a collection of religious hymns but also a source of profound philosophical insights. They plant the seeds of philosophical inquiry, ethics, and metaphysical speculation that would flourish in subsequent Vedic literature, including the Upanishads and the various schools of Indian philosophy. The Vedas' enduring significance lies not only in their historical importance but also in their role as a philosophical foundation that continues to shape the intellectual landscape of India and beyond.

- Urban planning and architecture

Urban planning and architecture in ancient India were characterized by remarkable achievements in city design, construction techniques, and architectural aesthetics. These aspects reflect the advanced urban civilizations that existed in the Indian subcontinent, particularly during the Indus Valley Civilization and later periods.

1. Indus Valley Civilization (circa 3300–1300 BCE):

- **Urban Planning:** Cities like Mohenjo-Daro and Harappa showcased well-planned layouts with grid-like streets, drainage systems, and standardized brick sizes. The streets were designed to allow efficient water drainage, a testament to their advanced understanding of urban planning.

- **Architecture:** Indus Valley cities featured two-story houses made of baked bricks, with rooms for living and storage. The Great Bath in Mohenjo-Daro is a notable architectural marvel, believed to have served ritualistic purposes.

- **Use of Materials:** The use of fired bricks in construction was a significant advancement. They were employed not only for buildings but also for creating complex drainage systems.

2. Vedic Period (circa 1500–500 BCE):

- **Architecture:** The Vedic period marked the emergence of more elaborate architectural structures. Temples and sacrificial altars were constructed using wood and stone, showcasing intricate carvings and designs.

- **Sacrificial Platforms:** Yajna (sacrificial rituals) played a central role in society. Elaborate altars known as "yajnashalas" were constructed to perform these rituals.

3. Maurya Empire (c. 322–185 BCE):

- **Architecture:** The Mauryan Empire, under the rule of Ashoka the Great, saw the construction of remarkable edifices like the Ashoka Pillars and stupas, most notably the Sanchi Stupa. These structures blended indigenous architectural styles with Hellenistic influences.

4. Gupta Empire (c. 320–550 CE):

- **Architecture:** The Gupta period is often referred to as the "Golden Age of Indian Architecture." Temples, monasteries, and cave complexes like the Ajanta and Ellora Caves exhibit exquisite rock-cut architecture and intricate sculptural work.

5. Chola Dynasty (c. 9th–13th centuries CE):

- **Architecture:** The Chola dynasty in South India made significant contributions to temple architecture. The Brihadeeswarar Temple in Thanjavur is an iconic example of Chola architecture, featuring a towering vimana (temple tower) and intricate stone carvings.

6. Mughal Empire (c. 16th–19th centuries CE):

- **Architecture:** The Mughal rulers introduced Persian and Islamic architectural influences in India. The Taj Mahal, built by Shah Jahan, is a masterpiece of Mughal architecture and renowned worldwide for its grandeur and beauty.

7. Rajput and Maratha Architecture:

- **Architecture:** Various regional kingdoms, like the Rajputs and Marathas, developed their unique architectural styles. Rajput forts and palaces, such as the Amber Palace in Jaipur, are known for their grandeur and intricate designs.

8. British Colonial Influence:

- **Architecture:** The British colonial period introduced a blend of European and Indian architectural elements. Iconic buildings like the Victoria Memorial in Kolkata and Mumbai's Chhatrapati Shivaji Terminus reflect this amalgamation of styles.

9. Modern Indian Architecture:

- **Architecture:** Post-independence India has seen the emergence of modern architectural trends. Architects like Le Corbusier and Charles Correa have left their mark with projects like Chandigarh and the Jawahar Kala Kendra in Jaipur.

The architectural history of India is a testament to its rich and diverse cultural heritage. It encompasses a wide range of styles, from the advanced urban planning of the Indus Valley Civilization to the grandeur of Mughal architecture and the regional nuances of Rajput and Maratha designs. This architectural legacy continues to influence contemporary Indian architecture, reflecting a deep connection between the past and the present. Indian urban planning and architecture have evolved over millennia, reflecting the cultural, technological, and societal changes in the subcontinent. The ancient Indus Valley Civilization showcased impressive town planning and drainage systems, setting early standards for urban organization.

Subsequent periods saw the rise of iconic structures like the rock-cut temples of the Gupta era, the majestic temples of the Cholas, and the architectural brilliance of the Mughals, exemplified by the Taj Mahal. Each dynasty and empire left a unique imprint on Indian architecture, blending indigenous styles with external influences. Modern Indian architecture continues to evolve, incorporating sustainable designs, cutting-edge technology, and contemporary aesthetics. This dynamic fusion of tradition and innovation is evident in structures like the Lotus Temple in Delhi and the Mumbai skyline's modern skyscrapers. Indian architecture serves as a bridge between the country's rich past and its promising future, a testament to its enduring cultural significance and adaptability.

Indian urban planning and architecture, spanning from the ancient Indus Valley Civilization to modern times, exhibit a diverse and culturally rich heritage. The meticulous city planning of the Indus Valley, the monumental creations of the Mughals, and the regional architectural wonders, all contribute to a tapestry of architectural marvels. In contemporary India, architectural design is driven by a blend of tradition and modernity. Architects draw inspiration from ancient architectural wisdom while integrating sustainable practices and innovative technologies into their designs.

Indian architecture serves not only as functional spaces but also as a means of preserving the nation's cultural identity, showcasing its creative expression, and adapting to the changing needs of society. Indian urban planning and architecture, spanning from the ancient Indus Valley Civilization to modern times, exhibit a diverse and culturally rich heritage. The meticulous city planning of the Indus Valley, the monumental creations of the Mughals, and the regional architectural wonders, all contribute to a tapestry of architectural marvels.

- Artifacts, symbols, and script of the Indus Valley people

The artifacts, symbols, and script associated with the Indus Valley Civilization offer valuable insights into the culture and society of this ancient civilization. While much remains mysterious about their script, many aspects of their material culture have been deciphered through archaeological discoveries.

1. Artifacts:

a. Pottery:

- Indus Valley pottery is characterized by its fine craftsmanship and a variety of shapes and sizes.

- Shapes range from simple to elaborate, including jars, vases, bowls, and pitchers.

- Pottery often featured intricate designs, including geometric patterns, animal motifs, and plant motifs.

- The use of a potter's wheel was prevalent, resulting in consistent forms.

b. Figurines:

- Terracotta figurines provide a glimpse into the daily life and religious practices of the Indus people.

- Common figurines depict animals like bulls, cows, and birds, possibly associated with religious symbolism.

- Some figurines represent humans engaged in various activities, such as dancing or playing musical instruments.

- Mother goddess figurines, often called "fertility figurines," have also been found, suggesting the veneration of a female deity.

c. Seals:

- Indus seals are some of the most iconic artifacts of this civilization.

- Made from materials like steatite (soapstone), these seals bear inscriptions in the undeciphered script of the Indus Valley.

- Seals often feature animals, mythical creatures, and human-like figures.

- They are believed to have been used for trade and administrative purposes, possibly as marks of authenticity on goods and documents.

d. Jewelry:

- Indus Valley jewelry includes necklaces, bangles, earrings, and beads made from materials like gold, silver, and semi-precious stones.

- Jewelry often featured intricate designs and craftsmanship.

- It is indicative of the aesthetic sensibilities and personal adornment practices of the people.

e. Tools and Implements:

- Tools and implements made from stone, metal, and bone

have been discovered, reflecting the craftsmanship and technological capabilities of the Indus people.

- Items include stone blades, metal tools, pottery wheels, and more.

- These artifacts point to a society with advanced skills in various crafts and industries.

f. Beads and Ornaments:

- Beads made from materials like steatite, shell, and terracotta were used for personal adornment.

- Ornaments such as bracelets, necklaces, and anklets were common, showcasing the importance of jewelry in their culture.

2. Symbols:

a. Animal Motifs:

- Animals such as bulls, cows, and rhinoceroses are commonly depicted on seals and pottery.

- These animals likely held cultural and religious significance, possibly representing deities or fertility symbols.

b. Plant Motifs:

- Plant motifs, including trees and various types of vegetation, are found in art and pottery.

- They may symbolize the importance of agriculture and the

natural world in the Indus Valley Civilization.

c. Human Figures:

- Human-like figures, often referred to as "priest-king" figures, are depicted on some seals.

- These figures are adorned with elaborate headdresses and garments and may represent individuals of high social or religious status.

d. Script Symbols:

- The script of the Indus Valley Civilization, which remains undeciphered, is composed of a set of symbols.

- These symbols are found on seals, pottery, and other artifacts.

- The script likely played a role in record-keeping, but its full meaning remains a mystery.

3. Script:

The script of the Indus Valley Civilization, often referred to as the Indus script, remains one of the most enigmatic aspects of this ancient culture. Key points about the script include:

- **Undeciphered:** Despite extensive efforts by scholars, the script remains undeciphered, meaning that the meanings of the symbols are not fully understood.

- **Writing Direction:** The script is typically written from right to left, but it has also been found in boustrophedon (alternating directions) style.

- **Usage:** The script is primarily found on seals, which suggests it may have been used for administrative and trade purposes.

- **Short Inscriptions:** Inscriptions are relatively short, typically consisting of a few characters.

- **Limited Corpus:** The total number of inscriptions discovered is limited, making it challenging to decipher the script based on context alone.

The script's mystery has intrigued scholars for decades, and while there have been various attempts to decode it, none have been universally accepted. The script's role in the civilization's administration, trade, and culture remains a subject of ongoing research and debate.

It is clear that the artifacts, symbols, and script associated with the Indus Valley Civilization provide valuable glimpses into the lives, beliefs, and practices of this ancient culture. While much about their script remains elusive, the material culture left behind reveals a society with advanced craftsmanship, artistic sensibilities, and a reverence for nature and possibly deities. These artifacts and symbols continue to be a source of fascination and exploration for

- Trade and cultural connections

Trade and cultural connections were vital aspects of the Indus Valley Civilization. While the civilization itself was centered around the fertile Indus River valley in what is now Pakistan and northwest India, it had extensive interactions with neighboring regions. Here's an overview:

1. Trade Networks:

- The Indus Valley Civilization engaged in long-distance trade networks that extended to regions like Mesopotamia (modern-day Iraq), Central Asia, and the Arabian Peninsula.

- Archaeological evidence, including seals and artifacts, suggests the presence of trade links with cities like Ur in Mesopotamia.

- Goods exchanged included textiles, pottery, metalwork, gemstones, and agricultural products.

2. Urban Centers as Hubs:

- Urban centers like Mohenjo-Daro and Harappa served as significant trade hubs, where goods were produced, collected, and distributed.

- A standardized system of weights and measures, evidenced by the discovery of standardized weights, facilitated trade.

3. Cultural Exchanges:

- Cultural exchanges were facilitated through trade routes, leading to the spread of artistic styles, techniques, and ideas.

- The seals of the Indus Valley, for instance, feature images of animals and deities that might have influenced religious and artistic motifs in neighboring regions.

4. Agricultural Diffusion:

- The Indus Valley's advanced agricultural practices, including the use of a sophisticated irrigation system, may have spread to neighboring areas.

5. Technological Exchange:

- The civilization's technological advancements, such as the use of fired bricks in construction and the potter's wheel, could have influenced neighboring cultures.

6. Decline and Dispersal:

- While the precise reasons for the decline of the Indus Valley Civilization remain debated, factors like environmental changes and the drying up of the Saraswati River may have prompted a dispersal of its people to other regions.

7. Legacy in South Asia:

- Elements of the Indus Valley Civilization's culture and practices likely contributed to the foundation of South Asian cultures, including the Vedic traditions and the subsequent development of Hinduism.

The Indus Valley Civilization was not isolated but engaged in extensive trade networks and cultural interactions with neighboring regions. These connections left an indelible mark on the development of early South Asian cultures and influenced the spread of technologies and ideas across ancient trade routes.

Chapter 3

Religion and Philosophy

The Indus Valley Civilization's religious and philosophical beliefs remain somewhat elusive due to the undeciphered script and limited textual records. However, archaeological findings and iconography suggest a reverence for nature and possibly a female deity, symbolized by mother goddess figurines. Their practices may have involved rituals and sacrifices. Over time, the cultural influences from the Indus Valley contributed to the foundation of early South Asian religious and philosophical traditions. The civilization's legacy likely played a role in shaping the religious and philosophical landscape of the Indian subcontinent, eventually giving rise to Hinduism, Buddhism, and Jainism, among others.

- **Evolution of religious thought: From polytheism to philosophical systems**

The evolution of religious thought in India is a complex and multifaceted journey that spans millennia. It encompasses the transition from polytheism to the development of intricate philosophical systems. This transformation is characterized by the emergence of major religious traditions, including Hinduism, Buddhism, and Jainism, each contributing unique philosophical perspectives.

1. Early Polytheism:

- In the Indus Valley Civilization, which existed around 3300–1300 BCE, there is evidence of polytheistic religious practices. Seals depicting various animals and deities suggest a diverse pantheon.

- The Vedic period (around 1500–500 BCE) saw the composition of the Rigveda, the oldest of the Vedas, which reflects polytheistic beliefs and the worship of numerous deities, including Agni (fire), Indra (thunder god), and Varuna (cosmic order).

- Rituals and sacrifices (yajnas) played a central role in early religious practices, aimed at appeasing deities and maintaining cosmic order.

2. Emergence of Philosophical Thought:

- Around 800 BCE, the Upanishads, a collection of texts within the Vedas, introduced profound philosophical ideas. They explored concepts such as Atman (the inner self) and Brahman (the ultimate reality), setting the stage for more abstract philosophical inquiry.

- The Upanishads questioned the efficacy of ritualistic practices and delved into the nature of reality and the self, marking a shift toward philosophical contemplation.

3. Hinduism:

- The evolution of Hinduism can be traced to the synthesis of Vedic traditions, Upanishadic philosophy, and the incorporation of regional and folk beliefs.

- The Bhagavad Gita, a key text within the Indian epic Mahabharata, expounds on moral dilemmas, duty (dharma), and the paths to spiritual realization.

- Hinduism encompasses diverse schools of thought, including Advaita Vedanta (non-dualism), Dvaita Vedanta (dualism), Yoga, and more. Each offers unique philosophical perspectives on the relationship between the individual soul (Atman) and the ultimate reality (Brahman).

4. Buddhism:

- Siddhartha Gautama, later known as the Buddha, founded Buddhism in the 6th century BCE. Buddhism emerged as a distinct philosophical and religious system in response to the prevailing Vedic and Brahmanical traditions.

- Core Buddhist teachings focus on the Four Noble Truths, the Eightfold Path, and the concept of Nirvana (enlightenment), emphasizing the cessation of suffering.

- Buddhism rejected the authority of the Vedas and the caste system, advocating a path to liberation accessible to all individuals, regardless of social status.

5. Jainism:

- Jainism, founded by Mahavira in the 6th century BCE, emphasizes non-violence (ahimsa), truthfulness, and asceticism.

- Jain philosophy centers on the concept of karma, reincarnation, and the pursuit of spiritual purity through renunciation and discipline.

- Jainism also challenged Vedic rituals and the caste system, advocating a path to spiritual liberation through self-control and moral conduct.

6. Later Developments:

- Over centuries, various philosophical schools and sects emerged within Hinduism, such as Nyaya (logic), Vaisheshika (atomism), and Mimamsa (ritual exegesis).

- Advaita Vedanta, founded by Adi Shankaracharya in the 8th century CE, became a prominent school of non-dualistic thought within Hinduism.

- Bhakti and Sufi movements emphasized devotion and personal connection with the divine, transcending ritualistic practices.

7. Syncretism and Coexistence:

- India's religious landscape has been marked by a degree of syncretism and coexistence. Many individuals and communities have drawn from multiple religious traditions and philosophical systems, creating a rich tapestry of beliefs and practices.

- The Bhakti and Sufi movements, for instance, promoted religious tolerance and unity, emphasizing the universal nature of divine love.

8. Contemporary Diversity:

- Modern India is characterized by a diverse religious landscape, with Hinduism, Islam, Christianity, Sikhism, Buddhism, Jainism, and others coexisting.

- Philosophical inquiry continues in various forms, with scholars and spiritual leaders offering interpretations and adaptations of ancient traditions to contemporary contexts.

The evolution of religious thought in India represents a dynamic journey from early polytheism to the development of intricate philosophical systems. This transformation has given rise to a diverse array of religious and philosophical traditions, each offering unique perspectives on the nature of reality, the self, and the path to spiritual realization. The coexistence of these traditions has contributed to the rich and complex tapestry of religious and philosophical diversity in India.

- **Major gods and goddesses in Hinduism**

Hinduism is a complex and diverse religious tradition with a vast pantheon of gods and goddesses. Many of these deities play significant roles in Hindu mythology, philosophy, and religious practice. Here are some of the major gods and goddesses in Hinduism:

1. Brahma:

- **Role:** Brahma is the creator god in Hinduism, responsible for shaping the universe and all living beings.

- **Attributes:** He is often depicted with four faces, representing the four Vedas, and four arms holding a scepter, a spoon, a book, and a lotus.

- **Worship:** While Brahma is one of the Trimurti (trinity) along with Vishnu and Shiva, his worship is relatively less common compared to the other two.

2. Vishnu:

- **Role:** Vishnu is the preserver and protector of the universe. He is believed to incarnate in various forms (avatars) to restore cosmic order whenever it is disrupted.

- **Attributes:** Vishnu is often portrayed with blue skin, holding a conch shell, a discus, a mace, and a lotus. His ten avatars, including Rama and Krishna, are central to Hindu mythology.

- **Worship:** Vishnu is highly revered, and devotees often worship him as the supreme deity, seeking his blessings for protection and sustenance.

3. Shiva:

- **Role:** Shiva is the destroyer and transformer of the universe. He is also associated with asceticism and spiritual realization.

- **Attributes:** Shiva is depicted with ash smeared on his body, a serpent around his neck, a third eye on his forehead, and a trident (trishul) in his hand. He is often seen in a meditative posture.

- **Worship:** Shiva's devotees, known as Shaivas, worship him in various forms, such as the Lingam (a symbol of his cosmic energy) and as Nataraja (the cosmic dancer).

4. Lakshmi:

- **Role:** Lakshmi is the goddess of wealth, prosperity, and fortune. She is associated with good luck and abundance.

- **Attributes:** Lakshmi is depicted with four arms, holding lotus flowers and showering coins. She is often seen seated on a lotus.

- **Worship:** Lakshmi is widely worshiped by Hindus, especially during the festival of Diwali, as her blessings are sought for material and spiritual prosperity.

5. Saraswati:

- **Role:** Saraswati is the goddess of knowledge, learning, and the arts. She represents creativity and intellectual pursuits.

- **Attributes:** Saraswati is often depicted playing a musical instrument, the veena, and holding a book and a lotus. She is associated with purity and wisdom.

- **Worship:** Saraswati is revered by students, scholars, and artists seeking her blessings for success in their endeavors.

6. Parvati (Durga/Kali):

- **Role:** Parvati is the goddess of power, love, and devotion. She is also known for fierce forms like Durga and Kali, representing the destructive aspect of the divine.

- **Attributes:** Parvati is often portrayed with a serene demeanor and two or more arms. Durga and Kali are depicted with multiple arms, holding weapons and standing on defeated demons.

- **Worship:** Parvati is widely worshipped, and her different forms cater to various aspects of devotion, from maternal love to fierce protection.

7. Ganesh (Ganesha):

- **Role:** Ganesh is the elephant-headed god of wisdom, knowledge, and obstacles. He is considered the remover of obstacles and the lord of new beginnings.

- **Attributes:** Ganesh is recognizable by his elephant head, potbelly, and four arms. He often carries a broken tusk, a modak (sweet), and a noose.

- **Worship:** Ganesh is invoked at the beginning of rituals and important life events to remove hindrances and ensure success.

8. Hanuman:

- **Role:** Hanuman is the monkey god known for his unwavering devotion to Lord Rama. He symbolizes strength, devotion, and loyalty.

- **Attributes:** Hanuman is depicted as a monkey-faced deity with a muscular body. He often carries a mace (gada) and is shown in a flying posture, holding a mountain.

- **Worship:** Hanuman is widely revered for his devotion and courage. His worship is particularly popular among devotees seeking protection and strength.

9. Krishna:

- **Role:** Krishna is a complex deity associated with divine love, charm, and wisdom. He is revered as a divine teacher and a key figure in the Mahabharata and Bhagavad Gita.

- **Attributes:** Krishna is often portrayed as a young, flute-playing cowherd with dark blue skin. He is also depicted as a warrior prince and diplomat.

- **Worship:** Krishna's worship takes various forms, including devotion to infant Krishna (Bal Krishna), Radha-Krishna love, and the philosophical teachings of Krishna in the Bhagavad Gita.

10. Radha:

- **Role:** Radha is the beloved consort of Lord Krishna and symbolizes divine love and devotion. She is revered for her selfless love for Krishna.

- **Attributes:** Radha is depicted as a beautiful woman often seen with Krishna. Her love story with Krishna is celebrated in Hindu literature, music, and art.

- **Worship:** Radha is worshipped as a symbol of pure devotion and the embodiment of love for the divine.

These are just a few of the major gods and goddesses in Hinduism, but there are countless other deities and divine manifestations, each with unique attributes and significance.

Hinduism's diverse pantheon reflects the multifaceted nature of the religion and its capacity to accommodate a wide range of spiritual beliefs and practices. The rich tapestry of Hinduism encompasses a multitude of gods and goddesses, each representing various aspects of the divine, human experience, and the cosmos. This vast pantheon reflects the diversity of beliefs, rituals, and philosophies within Hinduism. Devotees worship these deities for guidance, blessings, and spiritual realization, fostering a deep sense of connection to the divine. Whether seeking wisdom from Saraswati, strength from Hanuman, or divine love from Krishna and Radha, Hindus find spiritual solace and inspiration in the multifaceted expressions of the divine, which continue to shape their lives, culture, and traditions for millennia.

- **Concepts of karma, dharma, and moksha**

In Hindu philosophy, the concepts of karma, dharma, and moksha form a fundamental triad that underpins the understanding of life, ethics, and spiritual liberation. These concepts are central to the worldview of Hinduism and provide a framework for moral and metaphysical understanding.

1. Karma:

- **Definition:** Karma, derived from the Sanskrit word "kri," means "action" or "deed." It refers to the law of cause and effect, where every action has consequences.

- **Principle:** The principle of karma asserts that the universe operates on a system of moral and ethical causality. In other words, the consequences of one's actions are inextricably linked to those actions themselves.

- **Types of Karma**: Karma can be classified into three main types:

  - **Sanchita Karma:** The accumulated karma from past actions.

  - **Prarabdha Karma:** The karma from past actions that are currently being experienced in this life.

  - **Agami Karma:** The karma generated by present actions, which will have future consequences.

- **Influence:** Karma influences an individual's current life circumstances, experiences, and future rebirths (samsara).

- **Moral Significance:** Karma is deeply rooted in moral and ethical considerations. It emphasizes the importance of right conduct and responsibility for one's actions.

- **Role in Reincarnation:**

Karma is closely linked to the cycle of birth, death, and rebirth (samsara). It determines the nature of one's future lives, pushing the soul to evolve through successive incarnations.

2. Dharma:

- **Definition:** Dharma is a complex and multifaceted term with no direct English equivalent. It encompasses righteousness, duty, law, moral order, and ethical obligations.

- **Principle:** Dharma represents the moral and ethical duties and responsibilities that govern an individual's life. It is specific to one's age, caste, gender, occupation, and stage of life.

- **Dharma Shastra:** Dharma is expounded in ancient texts known as Dharma Shastras, which provide guidelines for virtuous living and ethical conduct.

- **Four Ashramas: Dharma is divided into four stages of life (ashramas):**

Brahmacharya (student life), Grihastha (householder life), Vanaprastha (retired life), and Sannyasa (renunciation). Each stage has its own set of duties and obligations.

- **Four Varnas:**

Dharma is also influenced by the four varnas (castes): Brahmin (priests and scholars), Kshatriya (warriors and rulers), Vaishya (merchants and farmers), and Shudra (laborers). Each varna has its dharma.

- **Moral Compass:**

Dharma serves as a moral compass, guiding individuals in making ethical choices and fulfilling their societal roles and obligations.

- **Relationship with Karma:**

Dharma and karma are closely intertwined. One's dharma guides their actions, and the quality of those actions (karma) influences one's future.

3. Moksha:

- **Definition:** Moksha, also known as "mukti" or "nirvana," is the ultimate goal of Hinduism. It signifies liberation from the cycle of birth and death (samsara) and the attainment of union with the divine or the realization of one's true self.

- **Principle:** Moksha is the highest state of spiritual realization, transcending worldly attachments and suffering. It represents the end of the cycle of reincarnation.

- **Paths to Moksha**: Hinduism offers various paths (yogas) to attain moksha, including:

- **Karma Yoga:** The path of selfless action and performing one's duties without attachment to the results.

- **Bhakti Yoga:** The path of devotion and surrender to a personal deity.

- **Jnana Yoga:** The path of knowledge and self-realization, often involving deep philosophical inquiry.

- **Dhyana Yoga:** The path of meditation and concentration.

- **Freedom from Suffering**: Moksha is liberation from suffering and the cycle of birth and death. It represents eternal bliss, knowledge, and union with the divine.

- **Realization of Atman-Brahman:** In some philosophical traditions, moksha involves realizing the identity of the individual soul (Atman) with the ultimate reality (Brahman).

- **Moral Transformation:** The pursuit of moksha often entails moral and ethical transformation, as one strives to overcome desires and attachments that bind them to samsara.

- **Role of Knowledge:** In many philosophical interpretations, knowledge and self-realization are central to attaining moksha, as they lead to the realization of the impermanence of the material world.

Interconnectedness of Karma, Dharma, and Moksha:

- Karma, dharma, and moksha are deeply interconnected in Hindu philosophy. The following points highlight their interdependence:

- Karmic Consequences:

One's actions (karma) have a direct impact on their adherence to dharma. Acting in accordance with dharma leads to good karma, while violating dharma results in bad karma.

- Dharma Guides Karma:

Dharma provides the ethical framework within which actions are evaluated. It guides individuals in making choices that align with righteous conduct, ultimately shaping their karmic outcomes.

- Moksha as the Ultimate Goal:

Moksha represents the ultimate liberation from the cycle of karma and samsara. To attain moksha, one must accumulate good karma through righteous actions and fulfill their dharma.

- Dharma to Moksha: Dharma serves as a means to achieve moksha by promoting ethical living and the pursuit of a virtuous life. Adhering to dharma helps individuals purify their karma and progress on the path to liberation.

- **Moral Evolution:** The cycle of karma, dharma, and moksha encourages moral and ethical evolution. Through righteous actions and adherence to dharma, individuals can elevate their consciousness and ultimately attain moksha. Karma, dharma, and moksha are foundational concepts in Hindu philosophy, providing a comprehensive framework for understanding life, ethics, and spiritual liberation. Karma governs the law of cause and effect, dharma guides ethical conduct and duty, and moksha represents the ultimate goal of liberation from the cycle of birth anddeath. These concepts are intricately woven together, shaping the moral and metaphysical landscape of Hinduism.

The journey towards moksha involves navigating the complex interplay between karma and dharma. Here's how these concepts work together:

1. Karma Influences Dharma:

- An individual's past karma influences their present circumstances, including their dharma. For example, the family, caste, and occupation one is born into are believed to be influenced by past karma.

- Dharma, in turn, guides one's actions and choices. It prescribes the moral and ethical duties that individuals must fulfill in their particular roles and life stages.

2. Dharma Shapes Karma:

- Adhering to dharma leads to the accumulation of good karma. When individuals perform their duties ethically and selflessly, they create positive karmic consequences.

- Conversely, neglecting or violating one's dharma results in the accrual of negative karma. Actions that harm others or disrupt the moral order generate unfavorable karmic outcomes.

3. Karma and Dharma Impact Reincarnation:

- The quality of one's karma directly affects the nature of their future rebirths. Good karma leads to a more favorable birth, while bad karma can lead to a less favorable or challenging birth.

- Dharma influences how individuals navigate their present life and accumulate karma, which in turn affects their future rebirths.

4. Moksha as Liberation from Karma and Dharma:

- The ultimate goal of moksha is liberation from the cycle of karma, dharma, and samsara. It signifies breaking free from the karmic cycle and achieving union with the divine or realizing one's true self.

- Attaining moksha involves transcending the constraints of karma and dharma, as one rises above the dualities and limitations of the material world.

5. Moral Evolution and Self-Realization:

- The interconnectedness of karma, dharma, and moksha encourages individuals to embark on a journey of moral evolution and self-realization.

- By acting in alignment with their dharma and accumulating good karma, individuals progress on the path towards spiritual awakening and liberation.

6. Paths to Moksha:

- While adhering to dharma and accumulating good karma is a valuable part of the spiritual journey, various paths (yogas) can lead to moksha. These paths include Karma Yoga (the yoga of selfless action), Bhakti Yoga (the yoga of devotion), Jnana Yoga (the yoga of knowledge), and Dhyana Yoga (the yoga of meditation).

7. Moral Responsibility and Spiritual Growth:

- The cycle of karma, dharma, and moksha underscores the moral responsibility of individuals for their actions and choices.

- It also emphasizes the potential for spiritual growth and transformation through ethical living, self-realization, and the pursuit of moksha.

In essence, karma, dharma, and moksha represent the intricate web of cause and effect, moral duty, and spiritual liberation that defines the Hindu worldview. This triad serves as a guide for individuals seeking to navigate the complexities of life, fulfill their ethical obligations, and ultimately transcend the cycle of birth and death to attain moksha

Why Moksha is the goal:

Moksha is considered the ultimate goal in Hinduism for several profound reasons:

1. Liberation from Suffering: Moksha represents liberation from the cycle of birth, death, and rebirth (samsara), which is characterized by suffering and the experience of worldly attachments and limitations. Achieving moksha means transcending these cycles of suffering.

2. Eternal Bliss and Knowledge: Moksha is often described as a state of eternal bliss, knowledge, and peace. It is a state of profound spiritual fulfillment and contentment beyond the transient pleasures and pains of the material world.

3. Freedom from the Cycle of Karma: In Hindu philosophy, the cycle of karma, where actions have consequences that bind individuals to samsara, is a fundamental aspect of existence. Moksha offers liberation from this cycle, freeing the soul from the bondage of karma.

4. Unity with the Divine: Moksha represents the realization of one's true self (Atman) as identical to the ultimate reality (Brahman), which is often described as the divine, infinite, and unchanging source of all existence. It is the merging or union of the individual soul with the universal consciousness.

5. Release from Ignorance: Moksha signifies the dispelling of ignorance (avidya) and the attainment of true knowledge and self-realization. It is the realization of the impermanence and illusory nature of the material world.

6. Ultimate Freedom: Achieving moksha is considered the highest form of freedom. It is freedom from desires, ego, attachments, and the limitations of the physical body. It is the freedom to exist beyond the confines of the material realm.

7. Purpose of Human Life: Hinduism teaches that human life is a precious opportunity for spiritual growth and self-realization. Attaining moksha is seen as the fulfillment of this higher purpose of life.

8. Break from the Cycle of Reincarnation: For Hindus, the cycle of reincarnation involves countless births and deaths, with each life presenting an opportunity to evolve spiritually. Moksha marks the end of this cycle, offering release from the necessity of further rebirths.

9. Ethical and Moral Transformation: The pursuit of moksha often entails significant moral and ethical transformation. As individuals seek to transcend worldly desires and attachments, they naturally cultivate virtues such as compassion, selflessness, and self-discipline.

10. End of Suffering: Hinduism acknowledges that human existence is fraught with suffering, which is attributed to desires, attachments, and the transient nature of the material world. Moksha promises an end to this suffering and eternal contentment.

It's important to note that while moksha is the ultimate goal in Hinduism, there are various paths (yogas) to reach this goal, and individuals may pursue it in different ways. Whether through Karma Yoga (selfless action), Bhakti Yoga (devotion), Jnana Yoga (knowledge), or Dhyana Yoga (meditation), the ultimate aim remains the same: to attain liberation from the cycle of birth and death and to realize one's true nature as part of the divine cosmic consciousness. Moksha represents the pinnacle of spiritual evolution and the highest realization of human potential in Hindu philosophy.

- Jainism and Buddhism: Founders, teachings, and impact

Jainism and Buddhism are two ancient Indian religions that emerged around the same time in the 6th century BCE. Both of these spiritual traditions share some common historical and philosophical roots, yet they also have distinct teachings and have left significant impacts on Indian and global religious and philosophical thought.

Founders of Jainism and Buddhism:

1. Jainism:

- **Founder:** Jainism is traditionally attributed to Lord Mahavira (Vardhamana Mahavira), who is considered the 24th Tirthankara or spiritual teacher of the Jain tradition. He lived around 599–527 BCE and was born in the same region as Siddhartha Gautama, who later became the Buddha.

2. Buddhism:

- **Founder:** Buddhism was founded by Siddhartha Gautama, also known as Gautama Buddha or simply the Buddha. He was born around 563–483 BCE in Lumbini, in present-day Nepal.

Teachings of Jainism:

1. Ahimsa (Non-Violence): Ahimsa is one of the core principles of Jainism. It emphasizes non-violence in thought, speech, and action towards all living beings. Jains are known for their strict vegetarianism and extreme care to avoid causing harm to any sentient being.

2. Anekantavada (Doctrine of Non-Absolutism): Jainism teaches that truth is multifaceted and that no single perspective can capture the complete truth. This doctrine encourages open-mindedness and respect for diverse viewpoints.

3. Aparigraha (Non-Possessiveness): Jains believe in minimalism and non-attachment to material possessions.

Aparigraha encourages simplicity and detachment from worldly goods.

4. Self-Discipline and Asceticism: Jain monks and nuns practice rigorous self-discipline, including fasting, meditation, and self-mortification. Asceticism is seen as a means to purify the soul and attain spiritual liberation.

5. Belief in Karma and Reincarnation: Jains believe in the concept of karma, where one's actions have consequences that affect future lives. Liberation from the cycle of birth and death (samsara) is the ultimate goal, and it is achieved through the accumulation of good karma and spiritual realization.

6. Concept of Soul (Jiva): Jainism posits the existence of an eternal and individual soul (jiva) that can attain liberation through spiritual practices and the shedding of karmic bondage.

Impact of Jainism:

- Jainism has had a profound influence on Indian culture, ethics, and philosophy. Its teachings of non-violence, truthfulness, and compassion have contributed to the development of a more ethical and compassionate society in India.

- Jain architecture, particularly the construction of ornate temples and intricate carvings, is a significant cultural legacy. Temples like those in Mount Abu and Dilwara are celebrated for their artistic and architectural beauty.

- The Jain concept of non-violence has influenced figures like Mahatma Gandhi, who adopted the principle of ahimsa in his non-violent struggle for India's independence from British rule.

Teachings of Buddhism:

1. Four Noble Truths:

- The First Noble Truth acknowledges the existence of suffering (dukkha) in life.

- The Second Noble Truth identifies the cause of suffering as craving and attachment (tanha).

- The Third Noble Truth presents the possibility of the cessation of suffering (nirvana).

- The Fourth Noble Truth outlines the Noble Eightfold Path as a guide to end suffering.

2. The Noble Eightfold Path:

- Right Understanding
- Right Intention
- Right Speech
- Right Action
- Right Livelihood
- Right Effort
- Right Mindfulness
- Right Concentration

3. Anatta (No-Self): Buddhism teaches the concept of anatta, which means there is no permanent, unchanging self or soul. This challenges the concept of an eternal soul and emphasizes the impermanence of all things.

4. Karma and Rebirth: Similar to Jainism, Buddhism acknowledges the concept of karma and reincarnation. However, the goal is to attain liberation from the cycle of rebirth (samsara) through enlightenment.

5. Meditation and Mindfulness: Buddhism places a strong emphasis on meditation and mindfulness as practices to gain insight, develop concentration, and ultimately attain enlightenment.

Impact of Buddhism:

- Buddhism has had a profound impact not only in India but also throughout Asia and the world. Here are some of its key contributions:

- **Spread Across Asia:** After its inception, Buddhism spread across Asia, influencing the cultures, art, and philosophies of regions such as Southeast Asia, Tibet, China, Japan, and Sri Lanka.

- **Art and Architecture:** Buddhist art and architecture have produced some of the world's most iconic and beautiful structures, including the stupas of India, the cave temples of Ajanta and Ellora, and the pagodas of East Asia.

- **Ethical and Philosophical Influence**:

Buddhism's emphasis on compassion, non-violence, and the pursuit of enlightenment has had a profound impact on ethics and philosophy. It has inspired individuals and societies to adopt more compassionate and ethical ways of life.

- **Dharma and Governance:** The concept of dharma, which originally appeared in Indian thought and was later refined in

Buddhist philosophy, has influenced governance and moral principles in various Asian societies.

- **Interactions with Other Religions:** Buddhism's interaction with other religions, such as Hinduism, Jainism, and later with Taoism and Shintoism in East Asia, has contributed to religious syncretism and the exchange of ideas.

- **Mindfulness and Psychology:** In recent years, the practices of mindfulness and meditation rooted in Buddhism have gained popularity worldwide. They have also been integrated into various therapeutic approaches and are recognized for their mental health benefits.

- **Secular Buddhism:** In modern times, some interpretations of Buddhism, particularly in the West, have embraced secular and humanistic approaches, focusing on meditation, ethics, and psychological well-being while minimizing the religious aspects.

- **Impact on Global Spirituality:** Buddhism's teachings on the nature of suffering, the impermanence of life, and the pursuit of inner peace and enlightenment resonate with individuals seeking spiritual meaning beyond traditional religious frameworks.

Both Jainism and Buddhism emerged in ancient India, offering unique philosophical and ethical teachings that have had a profound and lasting impact on Indian and global thought. While Jainism emphasizes non-violence, non-possessiveness, and the pursuit of spiritual purity, Buddhism centers around the Four Noble Truths, the Eightfold Path, and the quest for the cessation of suffering. Both traditions have left a rich legacy in terms of ethics, art, culture, and spirituality, influencing the way people perceive and engage with the world around them.

Role of Dharma is shaping Indian Culture:

Dharma plays a fundamental role in shaping Indian culture and society. It serves as a moral and ethical compass, guiding individuals and communities in their actions, responsibilities, and interactions. The concept of dharma is deeply ingrained in Indian culture and has had a profound influence on various aspects of life. Here's how different forms of dharma contribute to shaping Indian culture:

1. Sanatana Dharma (Eternal Religion):

-**Foundation of Indian Spirituality:** Sanatana Dharma, often referred to as Hinduism, forms the spiritual and philosophical backbone of Indian culture. It encompasses a vast array of beliefs, practices, and traditions that have evolved over millennia.

- **Pluralism and Tolerance:** Sanatana Dharma's inclusiveness and acceptance of diverse spiritual paths and beliefs have fostered a culture of religious tolerance and pluralism in India.

2. Raja Dharma (Duty of Kings and Rulers):

- **Historical Governance:** Raja Dharma, or the duty of kings and rulers, historically played a crucial role in shaping governance in India. It emphasized the responsibility of monarchs to protect their subjects and uphold justice.

- **Influence on Polity:** The principles of good governance, justice, and the welfare of citizens outlined in Raja Dharma have influenced the political philosophy and systems in India.

3. Grihastha Dharma (Duty of Householders):

- **Family and Social Structure:** Grihastha Dharma outlines the duties and responsibilities of householders, contributing to the structure of Indian families and society. It emphasizes family values, care for elders, and the importance of raising virtuous children.

- **Economic and Social Stability:** Grihastha Dharma encourages individuals to fulfill their economic and social responsibilities, promoting stability and harmony within communities.

4. Varṇa Dharma (Caste Duty):

- **Social Hierarchy:** Varṇa Dharma, which includes the duties associated with one's caste or varna, has historically influenced social hierarchies in India. While it has been a source of division and discrimination, it has also provided a framework for organizing society.
- **Contemporary Challenges:** Modern India grapples with the complexities and challenges associated with caste-based discrimination and strives for social justice and equality.

5. Yuga Dharma (Duty in Different Ages):

- **Cyclical View of Time:** Yuga Dharma recognizes that dharma may evolve or change in different cosmic ages (yugas). This perspective accommodates cultural shifts and adapts ethical principles to the changing times.

- **Adaptability:** The concept of Yuga Dharma allows for cultural adaptability while retaining core ethical values, ensuring that dharma remains relevant in evolving societies.

6. Svadharma (Individual Duty):

- **Personal Ethics:** Svadharma emphasizes an individual's duty based on their unique circumstances, talents, and roles. It encourages individuals to act in accordance with their own righteous path.

- **Self-Realization:** Svadharma is closely linked to the pursuit of self-realization and spiritual growth, contributing to the development of inner virtues and ethical consciousness.

7. Ahimsa Dharma (Duty of Non-Violence):

- **Non-Violence:** Ahimsa Dharma, rooted in the principle of non-violence, has had a profound impact on Indian culture. It promotes compassion, empathy, and non-harming of all living beings.

- **Influence on Social Movements:** Ahimsa played a central role in India's struggle for independence led by Mahatma Gandhi. It continues to inspire non-violent movements for social justice and human rights.

8. Dharma in Art and Literature:

- **Cultural Expression:** Dharma is a recurring theme in Indian art, literature, and performing arts. Epics like the Mahabharata and Ramayana, as well as classical dance and music forms, often explore moral and ethical dilemmas.

In conclusion, dharma, in its various forms, serves as a moral and ethical foundation for Indian culture. It influences the way individuals perceive their roles and responsibilities in society, guides governance, shapes family and social structures, and fosters ethical values. While dharma has evolved over time, it remains a critical component of India's cultural identity and continues to shape the nation's ethical and philosophical landscape.

- **Examination of the role of religion, philosophy, and spirituality in shaping ancient Indian culture.**

The role of religion, philosophy, and spirituality in shaping ancient Indian culture is profound and multifaceted. These elements have played a central role in influencing every aspect of life, from social norms to art, architecture, governance, and personal ethics. Here is an examination of their contributions:

1. **Religion:**

a. Hinduism:

- **Foundation of Indian Spirituality:** Hinduism, one of the world's oldest religions, laid the foundation for Indian spirituality. Its diverse beliefs, rituals, and practices encompass a wide range of philosophies and ways of life.

- **Social Order:** Hinduism's caste system, based on varna dharma, has historically structured Indian society and influenced social roles and occupations.

- **Sacred Texts:** Ancient texts like the Vedas, Upanishads, and Puranas contain spiritual and philosophical wisdom that continues to shape the spiritual consciousness of India.

b. Buddhism and Jainism:

- **Alternative Paths:** Buddhism and Jainism emerged as alternative spiritual paths in ancient India, challenging the prevailing Vedic traditions. They emphasized non-violence (ahimsa), compassion, and personal liberation.

- **Social Reform:** These traditions contributed to social reform by advocating for equality and non-discrimination.

2. Philosophy:

a. Vedanta: Vedanta, a philosophical system based on the Upanishads, explores the nature of reality and the self (Atman). It has inspired deep philosophical inquiry and discussions on metaphysics and the ultimate truth (Brahman).

b. Nyaya and Vaisheshika: These philosophical schools developed logical and epistemological systems, contributing to the advancement of analytical thinking and the understanding of knowledge.

c. Yoga and Samkhya: The philosophies of Yoga and Samkhya offered practical techniques for attaining spiritual realization and self-mastery. Yoga, in particular, has gained worldwide recognition for its emphasis on mental and physical well-being.

d. Charvaka: The Charvaka school represented materialistic and atheistic philosophy, challenging the prevailing spiritual beliefs. It encouraged skepticism and rationalism.

3. Spirituality:

a. Meditation and Mindfulness: The practice of meditation and mindfulness, deeply rooted in Indian spirituality, has gained global recognition for its therapeutic and psychological benefits. It promotes inner peace, self-awareness, and mental well-being.

b. Reincarnation and Karma: The concepts of reincarnation (samsara) and karma, found in various Indian religions, have influenced the belief in the interconnectedness of actions and consequences in life.

c. Bhakti and Devotion: Bhakti, the path of devotion to a personal deity, has been a cornerstone of Indian spirituality. It fosters emotional and spiritual connections with the divine and has produced rich devotional literature and art.

4. Impact on Culture:

a. Art and Architecture: Religious and philosophical themes have inspired some of India's most iconic art and architecture. Temples, sculptures, and paintings often depict religious narratives and philosophical concepts.

b. Literature: Ancient Indian literature, including the epics Ramayana and Mahabharata, as well as classical texts like the Bhagavad Gita, are imbued with spiritual and philosophical themes. They serve as moral and ethical guides.

c. Music and Dance: Indian classical music and dance have deep spiritual roots. They are used as mediums to express devotion and spiritual experiences.

5. Governance:

a. Dharmic Governance: The concept of dharma influenced governance in ancient India, emphasizing the responsibilities of rulers and their duty to uphold justice and protect their subjects.

b. Emperor Ashoka: Emperor Ashoka, a patron of Buddhism, played a pivotal role in spreading Buddhist principles of non-violence, compassion, and ethical governance.

Religion, philosophy, and spirituality have been integral to the development of ancient Indian culture. They have shaped moral values, social structures, art forms, and governance systems, leaving a profound and enduring legacy that continues to influence India and the world today. These elements remain at the core of India's rich tapestry of beliefs, practices, and philosophical insights.

- **Contributions of ancient Indian scholars to mathematics, astronomy, medicine, and other fields**

The contributions of ancient Indian scholars to various fields, including mathematics, astronomy, medicine, and others, have had a profound and lasting impact on the world. These scholars made significant advancements that laid the groundwork for further discoveries and continue to influence modern science and knowledge. Here, we discuss some of the key contributions and notable figures in each of these fields:

Mathematics:

1. Place Value System: Ancient Indian mathematicians developed the decimal place value system around 100 BCE. This system laid the foundation for modern numerals, making arithmetic operations more efficient.

2. Zero (Shunya): The concept of zero as a numerical placeholder was pioneered in India. Brahmagupta (c. 598–668 CE) was one of the first mathematicians to provide rules for mathematical operations involving zero.

3. Aryabhata: Aryabhata (c. 476–550 CE) made significant contributions to mathematics, particularly in trigonometry.

His work "Aryabhatiya" contains formulas for calculating the area of a triangle and the value of pi (π).

4. Brahmagupta: Brahmagupta, as mentioned earlier, contributed to algebra and introduced rules for solving quadratic equations. He also discussed negative numbers and their mathematical operations.

5. Bhaskara II: Bhaskara II (c. 1114–1185 CE) expanded on earlier work in calculus and provided solutions to various mathematical problems, including indeterminate equations and theorems related to planetary motion.

Astronomy:

1. Siddhanta: Ancient Indian astronomers developed Siddhantas, which were comprehensive treatises on astronomy and planetary motion. The "Surya Siddhanta" is one such important text.

2. Aryabhata's Model: Aryabhata proposed a heliocentric model of the solar system, where he correctly stated that the Earth rotates on its axis and the planets orbit the Sun.

3. Varahamihira: Varahamihira (c. 505–587 CE) made significant contributions to astronomy, including the prediction of eclipses and the study of planetary motion.

4. Jantar Mantar: Ancient Indian observatories, like the one in Jaipur (Jantar Mantar), showcased advanced instruments for measuring celestial positions and accurately predicting astronomical events.

5. Nakshatras: Indian astronomers divided the celestial sphere into 27 or 28 nakshatras (lunar mansions), which are still used in Indian astrology and navigation.

Medicine:

1. Ayurveda: India is the birthplace of Ayurveda, one of the world's oldest holistic healing systems. Ayurveda encompasses herbal medicine, diet, yoga, and other therapies to promote physical and mental well-being.

2. Sushruta: Sushruta (c. 600 BCE) is regarded as the "Father of Surgery." His treatise "Sushruta Samhita" contains detailed descriptions of surgical techniques, instruments, and procedures, including plastic surgery.

3. Charaka: Charaka (c. 300 BCE) is known for his foundational work in internal medicine. His "Charaka Samhita" is a comprehensive text on various aspects of medicine, including diagnosis, treatment, and pharmacology.

4. Ayurvedic Pharmacology: Ancient Indian scholars developed a sophisticated understanding of herbal medicine and pharmacology, which influenced the development of traditional medicine systems in Asia and beyond.

Science and Technology:

1. Metallurgy: Ancient Indians were skilled metallurgists. They developed advanced techniques for extracting and refining metals, including the production of high-quality steel known as "Wootz steel."

2. Water Management: The Indus Valley Civilization demonstrated remarkable expertise in urban planning and water management. They constructed intricate sewerage systems and planned cities with well-organized streets and buildings.

3. Textile Production: India has a long history of textile production, with ancient techniques for dyeing and weaving cotton and silk fabrics.

Philosophy and Epistemology:

1. Nyaya and Vaisheshika: These philosophical schools developed systems of logic and epistemology. Nyaya, for instance, codified rules of inference and argumentation.

2. Mimamsa: Mimamsa philosophers contributed to linguistic analysis and the study of rituals, influencing the development of Indian linguistics and ritual traditions.

3. Vedanta: Scholars like Adi Shankaracharya (c. 788–820 CE) promoted Advaita Vedanta, a non-dualistic philosophy that continues to be a prominent school of thought in Indian philosophy.

4. Yoga Philosophy: The ancient Indian sage Patanjali is credited with compiling the "Yoga Sutras," a foundational text on the philosophy and practice of yoga.

Literature and Linguistics:

1. Panini: Panini (c. 5th century BCE) composed the "Ashtadhyayi," a grammatical treatise that laid the foundation for Sanskrit grammar and influenced the study of linguistics worldwide.

2. Literary Epics: The Mahabharata and Ramayana are not only epic narratives but also storehouses of cultural, ethical, and philosophical wisdom.

Social Sciences:

1. Arthashastra: Kautilya (also known as Chanakya) composed the "Arthashastra," an ancient treatise on statecraft, economics, and political strategy. It covers a wide range of topics, including governance, diplomacy, taxation, and law enforcement.

2. Natyashastra: Bharata Muni's "Natyashastra" is a foundational text in the performing arts. It provides guidelines for drama, dance, music, and aesthetics, influencing Indian classical art forms.

3. Political Thought: Ancient Indian scholars, such as Chanakya and Shukracharya, contributed to political thought and governance systems that continue to be studied and debated.

Environmental Sciences:

1. Agriculture: Ancient Indian agricultural practices, including crop rotation and sustainable farming methods, have contributed to the preservation of fertile land and the promotion of eco-friendly agriculture.

2. Ecology: Ancient texts like the "Puranas" contain descriptions of ecosystems and ecological principles, reflecting an understanding of the interconnectedness of nature.

Social and Cultural Contributions:

1. Language and Literature: India's rich literary heritage, including classical works in Sanskrit and regional languages, has contributed to the development of world literature and storytelling traditions.

2. Music and Dance: Ancient Indian musical and dance traditions, such as classical music (Carnatic and Hindustani) and classical dance forms (Bharatanatyam, Kathak, etc.), continue to be celebrated for their cultural and artistic significance.

3. Spirituality and Yoga: India's spiritual traditions, including yoga, meditation, and mindfulness, have become global phenomena, influencing health and well-being practices worldwide.

4. Cuisine: Indian cuisine, known for its diverse flavors and use of spices, has gained international popularity, with dishes like curry, biryani, and samosas enjoyed globally.

5. Architecture: The architectural marvels of ancient India, including temples, stepwells, and palaces, continue to be admired for their intricate design and engineering.

6. Textiles: India's textile traditions, such as handwoven silk and cotton fabrics, have influenced global fashion and design.

7. Painting and Sculpture: Ancient Indian painting and sculpture, as seen in the Ajanta and Ellora caves and other sites, showcase artistic mastery and spiritual themes.

The contributions of ancient Indian scholars to mathematics, astronomy, medicine, and various other fields have left an indelible mark on human knowledge and culture. These achievements reflect India's rich intellectual and cultural heritage, and many of these ancient insights continue to be relevant and influential in the modern world. The legacy of these scholars underscores the significance of ancient Indian wisdom and its enduring impact on global civilization. The enduring contributions of ancient Indian scholars in mathematics, astronomy, medicine, philosophy, and numerous other fields continue to inspire and shape contemporary knowledge and practices. These achievements underscore the depth of intellectual thought and cultural richness that characterized ancient India. They remind us of the value of preserving and celebrating diverse cultural legacies as a source of global heritage. The wisdom of these scholars remains an integral part of India's identity and continues to inform modern science, philosophy, and spirituality. These contributions serve as a testament to the timeless pursuit of knowledge and the enduring impact of ancient Indian culture on the world stage.

Chapter 4:

Art, Architecture, and Urbanization

Art, architecture, and urbanization are intertwined facets shaping the visual and spatial landscapes of societies. Artistic expressions, from ancient murals to contemporary street art, reflect cultural identities and social commentary. Architecture, both historical monuments and modern structures, shapes urban environments, influencing lifestyle and community dynamics. Urbanization, marked by the growth of cities, necessitates thoughtful architectural planning and artistic integration for sustainable, aesthetically pleasing living spaces. Together, these elements weave a narrative of cultural evolution, societal values, and the dynamic interplay between human creativity and the built environment.

- Exploration of ancient Indian art forms, such as sculpture, painting, and literature.

Ancient Indian art forms, spanning sculpture, painting, and literature, embody the rich cultural tapestry of the subcontinent.

Sculpture:

Indic sculpture flourished across various periods and regions. The intricate carvings of temples, exemplified by Khajuraho and Ellora, showcase exquisite depictions of deities, celestial beings, and everyday life. Iconic sculptures like the Dancing Shiva and Yakshi sculptures demonstrate a harmonious blend of spirituality and aesthetics.

Painting:

Indian painting traditions are diverse and vibrant. The Ajanta and Ellora cave paintings, dating back to the Gupta period, depict vivid scenes from Buddha's life. Miniature paintings from Rajasthan and the Mughal era exhibit meticulous detail, capturing courtly life, nature, and mythological tales.

Literature:

Sanskrit literature forms the cornerstone of ancient Indian literary heritage. The Vedas, Upanishads, and epics like Ramayana and Mahabharata impart spiritual and moral teachings. Classical works like Kalidasa's "Shakuntala" and the plays of Bhasa showcase the sophistication of ancient Indian literary expression.

These art forms collectively offer a window into the cultural, religious, and philosophical dimensions of ancient India, illustrating a legacy that continues to inspire and resonate in contemporary times.

- Analysis of architectural marvels like the Ajanta and Ellora caves, temples, and stupas.

The architectural marvels of Ajanta and Ellora caves, temples, and stupas in India showcase the extraordinary craftsmanship and spiritual devotion of ancient artisans.

Ajanta Caves:

Located in Maharashtra, the Ajanta Caves date back to the 2nd century BCE to the 6th century CE. These rock-cut caves, primarily Buddhist, house intricate murals depicting scenes from the life of Buddha. The fusion of architecture and art creates a sublime environment, emphasizing the spiritual and artistic achievements of the time.

Ellora Caves:

Ellora, also in Maharashtra, is a UNESCO World Heritage site with structures representing Buddhism, Hinduism, and Jainism. Carved between the 5th and 10th centuries, the caves exemplify a synthesis of diverse religious traditions. The Kailasa Temple, a monolithic rock-cut marvel, stands as one of the largest and most awe-inspiring architectural achievements.

Temples:

Indian temples are diverse, showcasing various architectural styles and religious influences. The Khajuraho Temples in Madhya Pradesh, known for their intricate erotic sculptures, exemplify the artistic and architectural prowess of the Chandela dynasty. The Dravidian architecture of the Meenakshi Temple in Madurai and the intricate carvings of the Sun Temple in Konark also stand out.

Stupas:

Stupas, prominent in Buddhist architecture, serve as religious monuments and burial mounds. The Great Stupa at Sanchi, dating back to the 3rd century BCE, is one of the oldest stone structures in India. Its simple yet majestic design symbolizes Buddhist teachings, with intricate carvings depicting the life of Buddha.

Analysis:

1. Architectural Diversity: The diversity in architectural styles across these marvels reflects the rich cultural and religious history of India, showcasing the assimilation and coexistence of various traditions.

2. Spiritual Symbolism: Each structure, whether cave, temple, or stupa, carries profound spiritual symbolism. The intricacies of carvings and sculptures convey religious narratives and philosophical teachings.

3. Technological Ingenuity: The construction of monolithic structures like the Kailasa Temple at Ellora highlights the advanced technological knowledge of ancient builders, utilizing rudimentary tools to create intricate and colossal edifices.

4. Artistic Expression: The caves and temples serve as canvases for intricate artwork, illustrating stories, mythologies, and daily life. The integration of art and architecture demonstrates a holistic approach to cultural expression.

5. Cultural Continuity: These architectural marvels also signify cultural continuity, as many continue to be places of worship and pilgrimage, connecting the past with the present.

In essence, Ajanta and Ellora caves, temples, and stupas stand as testament to the ingenuity, spirituality, and artistic brilliance of ancient Indian civilizations, leaving an indelible mark on the architectural and cultural heritage of the subcontinent.

- Discussion of urban planning and the development of cities like Mohenjo-daro and Harappa.

The cities of Mohenjo-daro and Harappa, belonging to the ancient Indus Valley Civilization, offer fascinating insights into urban planning and development during the Bronze Age.

1. Advanced Urban Planning:

- **Grid Layout:** Both cities displayed an advanced level of urban planning with a grid layout of streets and well-defined neighborhoods. The streets were laid out in a precise grid pattern, showcasing a sophisticated understanding of city planning.

2. Well-Structured Infrastructure:

- **Drainage Systems:** Mohenjo-daro's intricate drainage system was an engineering marvel, with covered drains beneath the streets. This system exemplified a forward-thinking approach to sanitation, waste disposal, and public health, emphasizing the importance of urban hygiene.

3. Centralized Authority:

- **Centralized Administration:** The presence of large, well-planned structures, such as the Great Bath in Mohenjo-daro, suggests a centralized authority involved in city planning and public infrastructure. This indicates a level of governance and organization within these ancient cities.

4. Residential Planning:

- **Uniform Housing:** The residential areas featured uniform; multi-storied houses made of standardized bricks. This uniformity in construction materials and design suggests a planned approach to housing, possibly indicating a level of social equality or a standardized building code.

5. Economic and Commercial Hubs:

- **Marketplaces:** Both cities had well-defined marketplaces, indicating organized economic activities. The presence of granaries in Mohenjo-daro suggests a system for storing and distributing surplus agricultural produce.

6. Cultural and Religious Centers:

- **Citadel and Granary:** In Mohenjo-daro, the presence of a citadel and a granary suggests centers for administration and storage, possibly serving both economic and religious purposes. This integration of economic and religious functions reflects a holistic urban design.

7. Water Management:

- **Reservoirs and Wells:** The cities had advanced water management systems, including wells and reservoirs. The Great Bath in Mohenjo-daro may have served ritualistic or communal purposes, highlighting the cultural significance of water in these civilizations.

8. Fortification and Security:

- **City Walls:** Harappa was surrounded by massive walls, suggesting a concern for security. This defensive architecture indicates the need for protection and possibly centralized control over resources and trade routes.

9. Limited Evidence of Social Hierarchy:

- **Uniformity in Housing:** The uniformity in housing and absence of monumental structures associated with rulers suggest a society with limited evidence of extreme social hierarchy. This differs from many other ancient civilizations where monumental structures often indicated the power of rulers.

10. Decline and Abandonment:

- **Reasons for Decline:** The reasons for the decline of these cities remain speculative, with theories ranging from environmental changes to social and economic factors. The abandonment of Mohenjo-daro and Harappa adds an element of mystery to their urban histories.

Mohenjo-daro and Harappa represent early experiments in urban planning and governance, showcasing remarkable achievements in infrastructure, sanitation, and organization. The systematic layout of these cities serves as a testament to the sophistication of ancient Indus Valley civilizations and their contributions to early urban development.

- Influence of religion on art and architecture

Religion has wielded a profound influence on art and architecture throughout history, shaping cultural expressions and leaving an indelible mark on the visual landscape of societies. Here are key aspects of this influence:

1. Spiritual Symbolism:

- **Art as Devotion:** Religious art often serves as a form of devotion, visually representing spiritual beliefs and narratives. Icons, paintings, and sculptures become tangible expressions of the divine, fostering a deeper connection between worshipers and their beliefs.

2. Architectural Forms:

- **Sacred Spaces:** Religious architecture reflects beliefs in built form. Churches, mosques, temples, and synagogues are designed to create sacred spaces conducive to worship. Distinctive architectural elements convey theological ideas and cultural identity.

3. Ritualistic Purpose:

- **Functionality in Design:** Religious art and architecture are often designed with ritualistic functions in mind. Altars, prayer halls, and sacred images are positioned to facilitate religious ceremonies, creating environments conducive to worship and reflection.

4. Iconography:

- **Symbolic Imagery:** Iconography in religious art involves the use of symbols and imagery to convey specific meanings. Each element, from colors to symbols, carries religious significance, enabling the conveyance of complex theological concepts to a largely illiterate audience.

5. Cultural Identity:

- **Expressing Beliefs:** Religious art becomes a vehicle for expressing cultural identity. Styles and motifs in art and architecture reflect the specific religious traditions and beliefs of a community, contributing to a shared cultural and spiritual heritage.

6. Commemoration and Memory:

- **Religious Narrative:** Art and architecture serve as tools for commemorating religious events and figures. Murals, stained glass windows, and sculptures narrate religious stories, preserving and transmitting the collective memory of a religious community.

7. Inspirational Source:

- **Artistic Inspiration:** Religion has been a prolific source of artistic inspiration. The beauty of religious art and architecture often transcends the purely aesthetic, providing a source of inspiration and contemplation for believers and non-believers alike.

8. Influence on Urban Landscape:

- **Architectural Landmarks:** Religious structures often become iconic landmarks in cities, influencing the overall urban landscape. Cathedrals, mosques, and temples contribute to a city's identity and can serve as symbols of unity or markers of historical continuity.

9. Interplay with Rituals:

- **Integration of Rituals:** Architectural design and religious art often integrate with religious rituals. The layout of spaces, placement of religious symbols, and the use of light and sound contribute to the sensory experience of worship, enhancing the spiritual journey.

10. Dynamic Evolution:

- **Adaptation to Change:** Religious art and architecture evolve over time, adapting to changing cultural, social, and technological contexts. This dynamism reflects the continuous interplay between religious beliefs and the artistic expressions that convey them.

In essence, the influence of religion on art and architecture is a profound and enduring aspect of human culture. It not only shapes the aesthetic and spatial dimensions of societies but also becomes a means through which spiritual beliefs are communicated, perpetuating a dialogue between the sacred and the artistic.

Chapter 5

Economic Practices and Trade

Ancient India had a vibrant economy shaped by diverse economic practices and flourishing trade networks. Agriculture was the backbone of the economy, with advanced farming techniques, crop rotation, and irrigation systems. Trade routes like the Silk Road and the Spice Route connected India to the rest of Asia, Africa, and Europe. Valuable commodities such as spices, textiles, gemstones, and metals were exchanged. Coins like the punch-marked coins and gold dinars were used for transactions. India's economic prosperity influenced its art, culture, and society, making it a pivotal player in the global economy of ancient times.

- Analysis of the economic practices of ancient India, including agriculture, trade, and craftsmanship.

The economic practices of ancient India were diverse, dynamic, and influential, with agriculture, trade, and craftsmanship playing pivotal roles in shaping its economy. These practices were characterized by innovation, specialization, and connections to regional and international trade networks. Here, we analyze the economic landscape of ancient India in these key areas:

1. Agriculture: Agriculture formed the foundation of ancient Indian economy, with a rich history of practices that sustained a burgeoning population. Several factors contributed to the success of Indian agriculture:

a. Irrigation Systems: Ancient Indians developed sophisticated irrigation systems, including canals and wells, to harness the waters of rivers like the Indus, Ganges, and Yamuna. These systems allowed for year-round cultivation and increased crop yields.

b. Crop Diversity: Indian farmers cultivated a wide variety of crops, including rice, wheat, barley, millets, lentils, sugarcane, cotton, and spices like black pepper and cardamom. This diversity ensure food security and trade opportunities.

c. Crop Rotation: Ancient Indian agriculture practiced crop rotation to maintain soil fertility and prevent soil depletion. This sustainable technique allowed for consistent yields.

d. Agrarian Villages: The majority of the population lived in agrarian villages where they engaged in farming. These villages were largely self-sufficient, producing their food, textiles, and other essentials.

e. Guilds and Cooperation: Craftsmen and artisans formed guilds and cooperatives, which contributed to the development of specialized industries and trade in artisanal goods like textiles, pottery, and metalwork.

f. Land Ownership: Land ownership and taxation were well-documented in ancient India, with land grants to religious institutions, farmers, and administrators, facilitating land use and revenue collection.

2. Trade: Ancient India was a hub of trade activity, both regionally and internationally, with a well-established network of trade routes connecting it to various parts of Asia, Africa, and Europe:

a. Silk Road: India was a prominent part of the Silk Road, facilitating the exchange of goods, including silk, spices, gems, and textiles with China, Central Asia, and the Roman Empire.

b. Spice Route: India's spices, especially black pepper, cardamom, and cinnamon, were highly sought after in Europe and the Middle East, making the Spice Route a significant trade link.

c. Ports and Coastal Trade: Coastal cities like Muziris (modern-day Kodungallur) and Arikamedu served as thriving ports, facilitating maritime trade with the Roman Empire, Southeast Asia, and Africa.

d. Barter and Currency: While barter trade was prevalent, various forms of currency, such as punch-marked coins, silver dinars, and gold coins, were used for transactions, simplifying trade.

e. Cultural Exchange: Trade routes fostered cultural exchange, with India influencing art, religion, and philosophy in regions it engaged with, and vice versa.

f. Overland and Maritime Routes: Ancient India had a well-developed network of both overland trade routes, like the Grand Trunk Road, and maritime routes, connecting the subcontinent to distant markets.

3. Craftsmanship: Craftsmanship in ancient India was marked by remarkable skill and innovation across various domains:

a. Textiles: India's textile industry was renowned for producing high-quality fabrics, including fine cotton, silk, and wool. The weaving of intricate patterns, dyeing techniques, and embroidery were highly developed.

b. Metalwork: Skilled metalworkers crafted exquisite jewelry, coins, statues, and tools from materials like gold, silver, copper, and iron. The ancient art of metallurgy produced famous items like the Iron Pillar of Delhi.

c. Pottery: Pottery and ceramics were widespread, with diverse styles, including the distinctive red and black pottery of the Indus Valley Civilization.

d. Sculpture and Architecture: India's sculptors created magnificent temple sculptures and architectural marvels like the Ajanta and Ellora caves, showcasing intricate detailing and artistry.

e. Jewelry: The creation of jewelry, often adorned with precious and semi-precious stones, was a flourishing industry. Goldsmiths and gem cutters produced intricate pieces that were highly sought after.

f. Coinage: India's coinage evolved over time, with various dynasties and regions issuing their own coinage. These coins bore artistic designs and inscriptions, reflecting the culture and politics of the period.

Impact and Legacy: The economic practices of ancient India had a lasting impact on the region's history and culture:

1. Cultural Exchange: Trade networks facilitated the exchange of ideas, beliefs, and cultural practices. India's spiritual and philosophical traditions, including Hinduism, Buddhism, and Jainism, spread along trade routes.

2. Art and Architecture: Economic prosperity supported the creation of magnificent temples, sculptures, and art forms that continue to be celebrated for their artistic and cultural significance.

3. Technological Advancements: Ancient Indian metallurgy, textile production, and agricultural techniques laid the groundwork for future technological innovations.

4. Urban Centers: Thriving trade and economic activities led to the development of urban centers and cities, fostering social and cultural diversity.

5. Global Influence: India's commodities like spices, textiles, and gemstones were highly prized worldwide, contributing to India's recognition as a major global trading partner.

The economic practices of ancient India were marked by innovation, specialization, and interconnectedness. Agriculture, trade, and craftsmanship formed the pillars of a prosperous and culturally rich civilization. These practices not only sustained the livelihoods of ancient Indians but also left a profound legacy, influencing art, culture, and trade for generations to come.

The economic practices of ancient India not only sustained the civilization but also left an indelible mark on the region's cultural and historical landscape. These practices facilitated cultural exchanges, technological advancements, and urban development, contributing to India's rich heritage. The vibrant trade networks, including the Silk Road and Spice Route, connected India to distant lands, fostering cultural diffusion and the exchange of knowledge. India's role as a global trading partner introduced its unique cultural, artistic, and culinary contributions to the world.

The legacy of craftsmanship, seen in intricate textiles, metalwork, sculpture, and architecture, continues to inspire and inform contemporary art and design. Furthermore, the economic practices of ancient India set the stage for future technological innovations and the development of diverse industries. Overall, the economic practices of ancient India stand as a testament to the ingenuity and enterprise of its people, leaving an enduring impact on global history and culture.

- **Trade routes, both land and maritime, and their role in connecting ancient India with the rest of the world.**

Trade routes, both land and maritime, played a pivotal role in connecting ancient India with the rest of the world, fostering economic prosperity, cultural exchange, and the spread of ideas. These routes were instrumental in shaping India's history, influencing its culture, and contributing to its status as a global trading hub. Here, we delve into the significance and impact of these trade routes:

Land Trade Routes:

1. The Silk Road:

- **Significance:** The Silk Road was a vast network of interconnected trade routes that extended from China to the Mediterranean, passing through Central Asia and India. It facilitated the exchange of goods, ideas, and cultures between East and West.

- **Role in India:** Ancient India played a crucial role as a transit point along the southern branch of the Silk Road. Indian merchants traded spices, textiles, gemstones, and precious metals with travelers and traders from distant lands.

- **Cultural Exchange:** The Silk Road promoted cultural exchanges between India and other civilizations, including the Greco-Roman world. This led to the diffusion of artistic, religious, and philosophical ideas.

2. The Grand Trunk Road:

- **Significance:** The Grand Trunk Road, also known as the Uttarapath, was one of the world's oldest trade routes, connecting the Indian subcontinent from present-day Bangladesh to Afghanistan.

- **Role in India:** It served as a vital commercial and cultural artery, facilitating trade between different regions of the Indian subcontinent. Merchants transported goods like textiles, spices, and metals along this route.

3. The Spice Route:

- **Significance:** The Spice Route was a maritime trade network that connected India to Southeast Asia, the Middle East, and Europe. It was named for its role in transporting spices such as pepper, cinnamon, and cardamom.

- **Role in India:** Indian ports like Muziris (Kodungallur) and Arikamedu became significant hubs for spice trade, attracting traders from across the world, including the Roman Empire and China.

- **Cultural Exchange:** The Spice Route facilitated cultural exchanges and introduced Indian spices and textiles to foreign markets. It also influenced Indian cuisine and contributed to its diverse flavors.

4. The Incense Route:

- **Significance:** The Incense Route linked the southern Arabian Peninsula to the Mediterranean, passing through the western coast of India. It was named for the valuable incense traded along this route.

- **Role in India:** Coastal towns and ports along India's western coast, such as Aden and Ophir, served as intermediaries in the trade of incense, perfumes, and other luxury goods.

Maritime Trade Routes:

1. Muziris (Kodungallur) Port:

- **Significance:** Muziris, located in present-day Kerala, was one of the most prominent ports in the ancient world. It served as a major point of entry for goods coming from the

Mediterranean and was a center for trade in spices, gemstones, and textiles.

- **Role in India:** Muziris facilitated direct maritime trade between India, Egypt, Rome, and other regions. It contributed significantly to the economic prosperity of ancient India.

2. Arikamedu Port:

- **Significance:** Arikamedu, situated near modern-day Puducherry, was an important port for trade with the Roman Empire. Archaeological excavations at the site have revealed Roman artifacts, indicating active trade links.

- **Role in India:** Arikamedu served as a crucial center for the exchange of goods like beads, gems, and pottery between India and Rome.

3. Tamralipta (Tamluk) Port:

- **Significance:** Tamralipta, located in present-day West Bengal, was a bustling port on the eastern coast of India. It played a key role in maritime trade with Southeast Asia and China.

- **Role in India:** The port facilitated the exchange of goods like silk, tea, and other commodities between India and East Asia, contributing to India's economic ties with distant lands.

4. Barbarikon Port:

- **Significance:** Barbarikon, near modern-day Karachi in Pakistan, was an essential port along the western coast of the Indian subcontinent. It served as a significant gateway for trade between India and the Mediterranean.

- **Role in India:** Barbarikon was a hub for the export of textiles, gems, and spices to the Roman Empire. It was a crucial point in the Indian maritime trade network.

Impact and Legacy:

1. Economic Prosperity: The interconnected trade routes promoted economic prosperity in ancient India. The exchange of goods, including spices, textiles, gemstones, and metals, fueled India's economic growth and attracted traders from various parts of the world.

2. Cultural Exchange: Trade routes facilitated cultural exchanges, with travelers and traders bringing back not only commodities but also ideas, art, religions, and languages. Indian culture, particularly its spiritual and philosophical traditions, left a lasting impact on the regions it connected with.

3. Spread of Religions: Ancient trade routes played a pivotal role in the dissemination of religions like Buddhism, Hinduism, and Jainism to distant lands. Missionaries, scholars, and travelers carried these faiths along with their trade.

4. Technological Transfer: The exchange of knowledge and technologies occurred along these routes. India's advancements in metallurgy, textiles, and agriculture influenced neighboring regions and, in turn, shaped India's economy.

5. Culinary Influence: The trade routes introduced Indian spices and culinary traditions to foreign markets, contributing to the global popularity of Indian cuisine and its diverse flavors.

6. Architectural Heritage: The economic prosperity facilitated the construction of grand temples, palaces, and cities, with architectural marvels showcasing the wealth and creativity of ancient India.

Trade routes, both land and maritime, were vital conduits for connecting ancient India with the rest of the world. They fostered economic growth, cultural exchange, and the spread of ideas, leaving a profound legacy that continues to influence India and the global community to this day. These routes serve as a testament to India's historical role as a crossroads of civilizations and a hub of commerce and culture.

The trade routes of ancient India were not just conduits of commerce; they were pathways of cultural convergence, intellectual exchange, and technological diffusion. These routes linked India's rich heritage with the global tapestry of civilizations, leaving a lasting legacy. Through these trade routes, India shared its spiritual and philosophical traditions with the world, with Buddhism, Hinduism, and Jainism finding followers far beyond its borders. This cultural exchange influenced art, architecture, literature, and even governance systems in distant lands.

The economic prosperity these routes generated fueled India's growth, contributing to its scientific advancements, architectural marvels, and culinary innovations. Indian spices, textiles, and gemstones were highly prized commodities that introduced the world to the vibrancy of Indian culture. In sum, the trade routes of ancient India not only facilitated commerce but also facilitated the cross-pollination of cultures, ideas, and innovations, making them an enduring symbol of India's historical significance in the global arena.

- Coinage system and its implications for economic development.

The coinage system of ancient India was a fundamental component of its economic infrastructure, and its implications for economic development were profound. Coins served as mediums of exchange, units of account, and stores of value, fostering economic growth, trade, and stability. In this examination, we delve into the coinage system of ancient India and its far-reaching implications:

1. Origins of Coinage in Ancient India: The history of coinage in India dates back to around the 6th century BCE during the emergence of the Mahajanapadas (16 great kingdoms). Coins were initially made of silver and copper and were issued by various kingdoms to facilitate trade and tax collection. Over time, the use of coins became widespread and sophisticated.

2. Types of Coins: Ancient Indian coins exhibited a remarkable diversity in terms of materials, designs, and denominations:

a. Punch-Marked Coins: Among the earliest coins were punch-marked coins, typically made of silver or copper. These coins were stamped with symbols and marks, possibly representing weights or issuing authorities.

b. Silver Coins: Various kingdoms issued silver coins, often featuring depictions of rulers, deities, and symbols. These coins served as a medium of exchange in regional and international trade.

c. Gold Coins: Gold coins were considered symbols of wealth and were often issued by powerful empires. The Gupta Empire, for instance, issued gold coins known for their artistic quality and purity.

d. Regional Variations: Different regions in India issued their own coinage with distinctive designs and inscriptions, reflecting the cultural diversity of the subcontinent.

3. Economic Implications:

a. Facilitating Trade: The coinage system simplified trade by providing a standardized means of exchange. Traders and merchants could conduct business efficiently, leading to increased trade and economic activity.

b. Enhancing Tax Collection: Coins made it easier for rulers to collect taxes and revenue. The uniformity of coins facilitated the calculation and collection of dues, contributing to state finances.

c. Promoting Specialization: The availability of standardized coins encouraged specialization in various crafts and industries, leading to the growth of artisanal and manufacturing sectors.

d. Encouraging Economic Growth: A stable coinage system instilled confidence in economic transactions, fostering investments and economic development.

e. Wealth Accumulation: Coins allowed individuals to accumulate wealth, which could be invested in land, businesses, or other assets, further stimulating economic growth.

4. Cultural and Historical Insights: Ancient Indian coins provide valuable historical and cultural insights:

a. Iconography: The designs and inscriptions on coins often depicted rulers, deities, and significant events. These images offer glimpses into the political and religious beliefs of the time.

b. Dynastic Shifts: Changes in coin designs and inscriptions over time reflect dynastic shifts, historical events, and the rise and fall of empires.

c. Trade Routes: The discovery of ancient Indian coins in distant lands, such as Southeast Asia, the Middle East, and East Africa, attests to India's extensive trade connections and its influence on neighboring regions.

d. Artistic Expression: Indian coinage featured intricate artwork and calligraphy, highlighting the artistic prowess of the time.

5. Role in Religion and Rituals: Coins often played a role in religious and ritualistic practices:

a. Temple Offerings: Coins were commonly used as offerings to deities in temples, reflecting their significance in religious ceremonies.

b. Symbolism: Certain coin motifs, such as the "Lakshmi coin" depicting the goddess of wealth, symbolized prosperity and invoked blessings.

c. Rituals: Coins were used in various rituals, including weddings, festivals, and religious ceremonies, adding to their cultural significance.

6. Continuity and Evolution: The coinage system of ancient India evolved over the time to meet the changing economic and political landscape. Coins continued to be issued by various dynasties and empires, adapting to new technologies and materials. The Gupta coinage, with its gold coins featuring ornate designs, remains a testament to India's numismatic legacy.

The coinage system of ancient India was not merely a means of exchange but a dynamic force that shaped economic development, trade, culture, and history. Coins provided a standardized medium for transactions, promoted economic growth, and facilitated tax collection. They also served as historical artifacts, reflecting the artistic, political, and religious values of their time. The legacy of India's coinage system endures as a testament to its economic and cultural significance throughout history.

The coinage system of ancient India was instrumental in fostering economic development and shaping the cultural and historical fabric of the subcontinent. Its implications extended far beyond mere exchange and trade, encompassing broader aspects of society and civilization. Coins acted as catalysts for economic growth by providing a stable medium of exchange, which promoted trade and specialization. This, in turn, led to the development of artisanal and manufacturing sectors, as well as the accumulation of wealth, further stimulating economic activities Additionally, the coinage system offered valuable insights into the political, religious, and artistic dimensions of ancient India. Coin designs, featuring depictions of rulers, deities, and significant events, served as historical records. They also reflected the artistic prowess of the time, showcasing intricate artwork and calligraphy. Coins played a role in rituals and religious practices, symbolizing prosperity and invoking blessings. Their use in temple offerings and various ceremonies highlighted the integration of economic activities with cultural and spiritual aspects of life. Moreover, the continuity and evolution of the coinage system across dynasties and empires demonstrated its adaptability to changing technologies and materials. The Gupta gold coins, renowned for their artistic quality, stand as a testament to the enduring legacy of India's numismatic tradition.

In essence, the coinage system of ancient India was a multifaceted institution that transcended mere economic transactions. It played a pivotal role in shaping the socioeconomic, cultural, and historical landscape of the subcontinent, leaving a profound and lasting impact on India's rich heritage.

- Economic activities: Agriculture, handicrafts, trade guilds

In ancient India, economic activities were diverse and multifaceted, encompassing agriculture, handicrafts, and trade guilds. These activities played crucial roles in sustaining the economy, fostering specialization, and promoting trade and cultural exchange.

1. Agriculture:

- **Sustenance and Livelihood:** Agriculture was the backbone of ancient Indian society. Most of the population engaged in farming, cultivating a variety of crops such as rice, wheat, barley, millets, and pulses. This provided sustenance for the population and raw materials for other industries.

- **Innovative Techniques:** Ancient Indians developed innovative agricultural techniques, including advanced irrigation systems like canals and wells. Crop rotation was practiced to maintain soil fertility, contributing to sustainable farming practices.

2. Handicrafts:

- **Specialization:** Handicrafts thrived as artisans and craftsmen specialized in various skills, creating a wide array of products. Textiles, pottery, metalwork, jewelry, and woodcraft were among the flourishing artisanal industries.

- **Guild System:** Craftsmen organized themselves into guilds, known as "Shrenis" or trade guilds. These guilds regulated production, quality, and pricing, ensuring fair practices and providing a sense of community among artisans.

3. Trade Guilds:

- **Organization and Regulation:** Trade guilds were pivotal in the organization and regulation of trade and commerce. They brought together merchants, artisans, and traders engaged in similar businesses, fostering cooperation and mutual support.

- **Quality Control:** Guilds played a crucial role in maintaining quality standards. They set guidelines for production, ensured adherence to specific standards, and protected the interests of both producers and consumers.

- **Social and Welfare Functions:** Beyond economic functions, guilds had social and welfare roles. They provided support to members in times of need, organized festivals, and contributed to the well-being of the community.

4. Trade and Commerce:

- **Domestic and International Trade:** Ancient India had a vibrant trade network, both domestically and internationally. Domestic trade occurred within regions, facilitated by well-established trade routes and marketplaces. Internationally, India was connected to regions along the Silk Road, the Spice Route, and maritime routes.

- **Ports and Trading Centers:** Coastal cities like Muziris, Arikamedu, and Bharuch served as important ports and trading centers. These locations played a crucial role in facilitating maritime trade with the Roman Empire, Southeast Asia, and other parts of the world.

- **Commodities:** India was renowned for its valuable commodities such as spices, textiles, gemstones, and metals. The exchange of these commodities contributed significantly to economic prosperity and cultural exchange.

The economic activities of agriculture, handicrafts, and trade guilds were integral to the fabric of ancient Indian society. These activities not only sustained livelihoods but also contributed to the cultural richness and diversity of the subcontinent. The organization and regulation provided by trade guilds, the innovation in agriculture, and the craftsmanship in various industries collectively shaped the economic landscape of ancient India. Ancient India's economic activities were diverse, with agriculture as the cornerstone, providing sustenance and innovation. Craftsmanship thrived in textiles, pottery, metalwork, and jewelry, organized by trade guilds that regulated production and maintained quality standards. Trade guilds played a vital role in organizing commerce, fostering cooperation among artisans, and ensuring fair practices. The trade network, both domestic and international, facilitated the exchange of valuable commodities like spices, textiles, and gemstones, contributing to economic prosperity. Coastal cities such as Muziris and Arikamedu served as crucial ports, connecting India to the Silk Road and Spice Route. These economic activities not only sustained livelihoods but also enriched the cultural tapestry of ancient India, reflecting a harmonious interplay of agriculture, craftsmanship, and trade.

Chapter 6:

Social Welfare and Education

Ancient India placed significant emphasis on social welfare and education. Social welfare was often organized through the concepts of "dharma" and "charity," where individuals and rulers were encouraged to support the less fortunate through almsgiving and the establishment of hospitals and rest houses. Education was highly valued, with institutions like Takshashila and Nalanda serving as renowned centers of learning. Gurukuls, informal education centers, played a crucial role in imparting knowledge. The caste system influenced educational opportunities, but the pursuit of knowledge was seen as essential for personal and societal advancement in ancient Indian society.

- Discussion of the ancient Indian education system, including the role of gurukuls and universities like Nalanda.

In ancient India, the education system was a sophisticated and integral part of societal development, fostering intellectual growth, moral values, and professional skills. Gurukuls and universities like Nalanda played pivotal roles in shaping the educational landscape.

Gurukuls:

1. Traditional Centers of Learning:
Gurukuls were traditional residential schools where students lived with their teachers, imbibing knowledge through close mentorship.

2. Structure and Curriculum:
- Gurukuls were typically situated in serene, natural surroundings conducive to learning.
- The curriculum was comprehensive, encompassing the Vedas, scriptures, philosophy, grammar, mathematics, astronomy, and physical education.

3. Guru-Shishya Parampara:
- The guru (teacher) held a revered position, guiding students not only academically but also in ethical and moral principles.
- Students, known as shishyas, lived in close-knit communities, fostering a sense of familial bonds and respect for elders.

4. Oral Tradition:
- Emphasis was placed on oral transmission of knowledge, encouraging memorization and recitation of sacred texts.
- Rigorous discipline and adherence to a code of conduct

were integral aspects of gurukul education.

5. Holistic Development:

- Education aimed at holistic development, encompassing physical fitness, ethical behavior, and intellectual prowess.
- Practical skills were imparted through hands-on experiences, aligning education with real-life applications.

6. Individualized Learning:

- The guru tailored the education to the individual needs and abilities of each student, recognizing diverse aptitudes.

7. Spiritual and Cultural Integration:

- Gurukuls played a crucial role in preserving and transmitting cultural and spiritual heritage.
- Rituals, festivals, and storytelling were integrated into the educational process to instill a sense of cultural identity.

8. Duration of Education:

- The duration of education in a gurukul was flexible, with students often staying for extended periods to master various subjects.

Universities like Nalanda:

1. Establishing Centers of Higher Learning:

- Nalanda, founded in the 5th century CE, was one of the most renowned universities in ancient India.
- Universities like Nalanda and Takshashila attracted scholars from various parts of the world.

2. Academic Excellence:

- Nalanda offered a vast curriculum, including subjects like philosophy, theology, medicine, astronomy, mathematics, and logic.
- Scholars at Nalanda engaged in research, contributing to advancements in various fields.

3. International Recognition:

- Nalanda gained international acclaim, attracting students and scholars from China, Tibet, Korea, and Central Asia.
- Its reputation as a center of excellence extended beyond Indian borders.

4. Library and Manuscripts:

- Nalanda housed a massive library, considered one of the largest repositories of knowledge in the ancient world.
- Manuscripts in multiple languages were meticulously preserved, fostering a culture of intellectual exploration.

5. Residential Complex:

- Nalanda was a residential university with dormitories, lecture halls, meditation chambers, and gardens, creating a conducive environment for learning.

6. Rigorous Academic Standards:

- Admission to Nalanda was highly competitive, emphasizing merit-based selection.
- Rigorous examinations ensured academic standards and intellectual rigor.

7. Cultural Exchange:

- The presence of scholars from diverse backgrounds

facilitated cultural exchange and the synthesis of ideas.

- Nalanda's influence extended to Southeast Asia, where its teachings left a lasting impact.

8. Decline and Destruction:

- Nalanda faced decline and eventual destruction during invasions in the 12th century, marking the end of a glorious era in Indian education.

Impact and Legacy:

1. Intellectual Legacy:

- The Gurukul system and institutions like Nalanda laid the foundation for India's intellectual legacy, influencing subsequent educational traditions.

2. Cultural Preservation:

- Gurukuls played a vital role in preserving and transmitting cultural and spiritual values, ensuring continuity across generations.

3. Global Recognition:

- The international recognition of universities like Nalanda highlights India's historical position as a global center for learning.

4. Inspirational Models:

- The gurukul model continues to inspire modern educational approaches that emphasize personalized learning and holistic development.

5. Cultural Identity:

- Gurukuls and ancient universities contributed to the shaping of India's cultural identity, fostering a sense of pride in its intellectual and spiritual heritage.

The ancient Indian education system, epitomized by gurukuls and universities like Nalanda, was a testament to the country's commitment to knowledge, holistic development, and cultural preservation. These institutions fostered an environment where education went beyond rote learning, emphasizing critical thinking, moral values, and the synthesis of diverse fields. The legacy of this system endures, influencing contemporary educational philosophies and contributing to the rich tapestry of India's cultural and intellectual heritage.

- Exploration of social welfare measures, including healthcare, charity, and support for marginalized communities.

In ancient India, social welfare was a cornerstone of societal values, manifesting through a variety of measures aimed at promoting well-being, healthcare, charity, and support for marginalized communities. These initiatives were deeply rooted in the cultural, religious, and ethical fabric of the society, reflecting a commitment to compassion and communal harmony.

1. Healthcare:

a. Ayurveda:

- Ayurveda, the ancient Indian system of medicine, played a crucial role in healthcare.
- Physicians, known as Vaidyas, practiced Ayurvedic

principles, emphasizing a holistic approach to well-being.

b. Hospitals and Infirmary:

- Ancient India had well-established hospitals and infirmaries. For example, during the Mauryan period, Emperor Ashoka is believed to have built hospitals for humans and animals.
- These institutions provided medical care, surgery, and therapeutic treatments.

c. Herbal Remedies:

- Ayurveda extensively utilized herbal remedies, promoting the use of medicinal plants for various ailments.
- Communities often had herbal gardens, and knowledge of herbal medicine was shared among healers.

d. Yoga and Meditation:

- Yoga and meditation were integral to health and well-being. Yogic practices focused on physical, mental, and spiritual balance.
- Monastic orders, such as those established by Adi Shankaracharya, emphasized yoga for holistic health.

2. Charity and Philanthropy:

a. Dāna (Charity):

- The concept of dāna, or charity, was deeply ingrained in Indian society. Individuals and rulers were encouraged to give generously to those in need.

- Charity extended to providing food, clothing, shelter, and financial support to the less fortunate.

b. Construction of Rest Houses and Wells:

- Kings and wealthy individuals sponsored the construction of rest houses (dharmashalas) and wells along trade routes.
- These facilities served travelers, pilgrims, and the general public, showcasing a commitment to public welfare.

c. Feeding the Poor:

- Annadana, the act of feeding the poor, was considered a noble deed. Temples and wealthy households organized community meals, providing sustenance to the hungry.

d. Support for Education:

- Donations were made to educational institutions, particularly gurukuls and universities, to ensure the dissemination of knowledge.
- Wealthy patrons supported scholars and students, contributing to the advancement of learning.

3. Support for Marginalized Communities:

a. Empowerment of Women:

- Ancient India witnessed efforts to empower women through education and social initiatives.
- Women like Gargi and Maitreyi were revered scholars, contributing to philosophical and intellectual discourse.

b. Welfare for Widows and Orphans:

- Special attention was given to the welfare of widows and orphans. Charitable institutions and individuals provided support and protection to those in vulnerable circumstances.

c. Upliftment of the Downtrodden:

- Efforts were made to uplift marginalized communities, such as the Scheduled Castes (Dalits). Social reformers advocated for their rights and dignity.

d. Religious Tolerance:

- The concept of religious tolerance was embedded in social welfare. Different religious communities coexisted, and rulers often patronized multiple faiths.
- Emperors like Akbar promoted religious harmony through policies like Din-i Ilahi.

4. Legal and Ethical Frameworks:

a. Dharmashastra:

- Dharmashastra, ancient legal and ethical texts, provided guidelines for social conduct and justice.
- These texts emphasized the importance of righteous governance and protection of the vulnerable.

b. Rule of Law:

- Kings were expected to uphold dharma, ensuring a just and equitable society.
- Legal systems addressed disputes, and rulers were advised to provide fair and impartial judgments.

c. Protection of Animals:

- Ancient India displayed concern for animal welfare. Laws were enacted to protect animals from cruelty.
- Initiatives such as the establishment of shelters for injured animals reflected a compassionate approach.

5. Religious and Cultural Practices:

a. Pilgrimages and Religious Festivals:

- Pilgrimages were not only spiritual journeys but also opportunities for social welfare. Pilgrims often engaged in acts of charity and service along their routes.
- Religious festivals included community-oriented activities, such as feeding the hungry and supporting the needy.

b. Social Festivals and Celebrations:

- Social festivals, like Diwali, were occasions for sharing joy and prosperity with others.
- Wealthy individuals sponsored community celebrations, fostering a sense of unity and well-being.

c. Social Codes of Conduct:

- Manusmriti and other ancient texts outlined social codes of conduct. These codes emphasized duties towards family, community, and society at large.
- Acts of kindness and charity were integral to fulfilling one's societal obligations.

6. Challenges and Evolutions:

a. Decline of Social Welfare Practices:

- With invasions and political changes, some social welfare practices faced decline, leading to the erosion of certain traditions.

b. Adaptation to Changing Circumstances:

- However, the essence of social welfare adapted to changing circumstances. Later rulers and communities continued to uphold charitable and philanthropic activities.

c. Resurgence in the Medieval Period:

- During the medieval period, rulers like Akbar and others continued to implement social welfare measures, ensuring the well-being of their subjects.

d. Modern Social Welfare Movements:

- Social reform movements in the 19th and 20th centuries, led by figures like Raja Ram Mohan Roy and Mahatma Gandhi, aimed at addressing social inequalities and promoting welfare.

Ancient India's commitment to social welfare, encompassing healthcare, charity, and support for marginalized communities, was rooted in a holistic understanding of societal well-being. These practices were not isolated acts of charity but were deeply embedded in cultural, religious, and ethical frameworks. The legacy of these initiatives endures, influencing contemporary notions of philanthropy, social responsibility, and compassionate governance. Recognizing the historical roots of social welfare in ancient India provides valuable insights for shaping inclusive and compassionate societies in the present and future. Ancient India's commitment to social welfare, evident through healthcare, charity, and support for marginalized communities, epitomized a holistic approach to well-being. The foundations laid by initiatives like Ayurveda, dāna, and the empowerment of marginalized groups were integral to the cultural and ethical fabric. While facing challenges and transformations over time, these practices left an indelible mark on the nation's social consciousness. The enduring legacy of ancient India's social welfare measures continues to inspire contemporary efforts, emphasizing the importance of compassion, inclusivity, and the collective responsibility of society for the welfare of all its members.

- **Analysis of the contribution of education and social welfare to the overall development of the society.**

The contribution of education and social welfare to the overall development of society is profound, shaping not only individual lives but also the collective fabric of communities and nations. In ancient India, the synergistic relationship between education and social welfare played a pivotal role in fostering holistic development. This analysis explores how these two pillars have been instrumental in shaping societies, impacting cultural values, economic progress, and the well-being of individuals.

1. Education as a Catalyst for Societal Development:

a. Intellectual Advancements:

- Education serves as the bedrock for intellectual advancements, fostering critical thinking, creativity, and innovation.

- Ancient Indian educational institutions, such as gurukuls

and universities like Nalanda, were hubs of intellectual exploration, contributing to advancements in philosophy, science, and literature.

b. Preservation and Transmission of Culture:

- Education has been a key agent in preserving and transmitting cultural heritage from one generation to the next.

- Gurukuls, through their oral traditions and rigorous study of scriptures, played a vital role in safeguarding and passing on cultural values, rituals, and traditions.

c. Ethical and Moral Development:

- Education is not merely about acquiring knowledge but also about fostering ethical and moral development.

- Ancient Indian education, deeply rooted in principles like dharma, aimed at instilling values of righteousness, compassion, and social responsibility.

d. Social Cohesion and Harmony:

- Education promotes social cohesion by bringing diverse communities together through shared knowledge and understanding.

- Gurukuls, where students from different backgrounds lived and studied together, exemplified the role of education in fostering communal harmony.

e. Skill Development and Specialization:

- Education equips individuals with the skills necessary for professional and personal development.

- Ancient Indian education, especially in gurukuls, emphasized not only academic knowledge but also practical skills, including craftsmanship, medicine, and astronomy.

f. Empowerment of Marginalized Groups:

- Education has the potential to empower marginalized groups by providing them with opportunities for socio-economic mobility.

- Ancient India saw instances of women like Gargi and Maitreyi participating in scholarly pursuits, challenging gender norms and contributing to societal progress.

2. Social Welfare as a Pillar of Societal Development:

a. Health and Well-being:

- Social welfare measures, particularly in healthcare, are fundamental for the well-being of society.

- Ayurveda, supported by charitable initiatives and hospitals, contributed to the overall health of communities in ancient India.

b. Economic Prosperity:

- Social welfare, including charity and philanthropy, has a direct impact on economic prosperity.

- Acts of dāna (charity) supported the less fortunate, contributing to social and economic balance.

c. Social Equity and Inclusion:

- Social welfare initiatives aim to create a more equitable and inclusive society.

- In ancient India, the construction of rest houses, support for widows and orphans, and protection of marginalized groups reflected a commitment to social equity.

d. Legal and Ethical Frameworks:

- Social welfare is often intertwined with legal and ethical frameworks that govern a society.

- Ancient legal texts like Dharmashastra provided guidelines for rulers to ensure justice, protection of the vulnerable, and ethical governance.

e. Cultural Preservation:

- Social welfare initiatives contribute to the preservation of cultural values by ensuring the well-being of communities.

- Festivals, community celebrations, and charitable acts were not just social events but integral to preserving the cultural identity of ancient Indian society.

3. Synergy Between Education and Social Welfare:

a. Education as a Driver of Social Welfare:

- An educated society is more likely to engage in social welfare activities due to increased awareness and empathy.

- Scholars and educated individuals in ancient India often took active roles in charitable endeavors, supporting education, healthcare, and community well-being.

b. Social Welfare Enhancing Access to Education:

- Social welfare measures, such as support for education, can break down barriers to access and promote inclusivity.

- Charitable donations often went towards funding gurukuls and universities, ensuring educational opportunities for a broader segment of society.

c. Holistic Development:

- The combination of education and social welfare fosters holistic development by addressing both intellectual and socio-economic dimensions.

- Gurukuls, where education was not limited to academics but included ethical and practical learning, exemplify the holistic approach to development.

d. Empowerment Through Education and Social Welfare:

- The empowerment of marginalized groups is a shared goal of both education and social welfare.

- Education provides the tools for empowerment, while social welfare measures create an enabling environment for marginalized individuals to thrive.

4. Challenges and Evolutions:

a. Changing Societal Dynamics:

- The dynamic interplay between education and social welfare has faced challenges with changing societal structures and values.

- As societies evolve, new approaches are needed to address emerging issues and disparities.

b. Modernization and Technology:

- Modernization and technological advancements have reshaped education and social welfare.

- While technology can enhance educational access, it also poses challenges in terms of equity and the digital divide.

c. Globalization and Cultural Influences:

- Globalization brings diverse cultural influences, impacting both education and social welfare.
- Societies must navigate a balance between preserving cultural values and adapting to global changes.

d. Policy and Governance:

- Effective policies and governance play a crucial role in ensuring the harmonious integration of education and social welfare.

- Governments need to create frameworks that support inclusive education and equitable social welfare measures.

5. Contemporary Relevance:

a. Modern Education Systems:

- Modern education systems aim to combine academic excellence with holistic development.

- Concepts like value-based education and experiential learning echo the ancient Indian emphasis on holistic development.

b. Social Welfare in the 21st Century:

- Contemporary social welfare initiatives focus on inclusivity, sustainability, and addressing global challenges.

- The United Nations Sustainable Development Goals (SDGs) embody a modern approach to global social welfare.

c. Educational and Social Innovations:

- Innovations in education and social welfare leverage technology, research, and community engagement.
- Initiatives like online education platforms and social entrepreneurship reflect contemporary approaches to societal development.

Both education and social welfare in ancient India laid the foundations for holistic societal development. Education, as a catalyst for intellectual and ethical growth, synergized with social welfare measures that addressed health, economic balance, and social equity. The dynamic relationship between these pillars created a harmonious society that valued knowledge, compassion, and collective well-being. As societies evolve, the principles established by ancient India's educational and social welfare systems remain relevant. The lessons learned from this historical analysis provide insights for contemporary challenges, emphasizing the need for inclusive education, equitable social welfare measures, and the integration of cultural values into societal development. Striking a balance between educational excellence and compassionate social welfare continues to be essential for fostering sustainable, inclusive, and harmonious societies in the present and future.

Chapter 7

Literature and Language

Literature and language are integral components of cultural identity, shaping the tapestry of societies. In ancient India, a rich literary tradition flourished, encompassing epics like the Mahabharata and Ramayana, philosophical texts like the Upanishads, and treatises on science, medicine, and arts. Sanskrit, the classical language, served as a vehicle for these profound works. The oral tradition, epitomized by the Vedas, added a dynamic layer to literary transmission. Literature not only reflected societal values but also played a role in moral education. Today, the diverse languages and literature of India continue to contribute to the nation's cultural mosaic, fostering a deep connection to its ancient roots.

- The development of Sanskrit as a classical language

Sanskrit, recognized as one of the oldest classical languages in the world, underwent a fascinating development, leaving an indelible mark on the cultural and literary heritage of ancient India. Its evolution is a testament to the intellectual vigor of the civilization that fostered it, reflecting the intricate interplay of linguistic, cultural, and philosophical influences.

The roots of Sanskrit can be traced to the Vedic period, approximately around 1500 BCE. The Vedic texts, composed in an early form of Sanskrit known as Vedic Sanskrit, constitute the oldest layer of Indian literature. These texts, including the Rigveda, Samaveda, Yajurveda, and Atharvaveda, were transmitted orally for centuries before being systematically compiled.

Over time, linguistic developments occurred, leading to the emergence of Classical Sanskrit. The linguistic sophistication of Classical Sanskrit is exemplified by the grammarian Panini's work, "Ashtadhyayi," composed around the 4th century BCE. Panini's grammar provided a systematic and comprehensive framework for the language, outlining rules governing morphology, syntax, and semantics. This foundational work not only standardized Sanskrit but also laid the groundwork for linguistic analysis, influencing subsequent linguistic studies globally.

The transition to Classical Sanskrit marked a shift from the fluid and evolving language of the Vedas to a more refined, systematic, and grammatically precise form. This standardization was essential for the transmission of religious, philosophical, and scientific knowledge, facilitating a uniform language of discourse across diverse regions.

Sanskrit's development as a classical language was closely intertwined with its role as the vehicle for religious and philosophical discourse. The Upanishads, dating from around the 8th to 6th centuries BCE, engaged in profound philosophical inquiries and discussions, expressing complex ideas with linguistic precision. The Bhagavad Gita, embedded within the Indian epic Mahabharata, further exemplifies the literary and philosophical heights achieved by Sanskrit during this period.

The significance of Sanskrit extended beyond religious and philosophical contexts. It became the language of classical literature, encompassing a vast and varied corpus of texts. The epics, Mahabharata and Ramayana, stand as monumental works of Sanskrit literature, combining narrative richness with moral and philosophical depth. Kalidasa, often hailed as the "Shakespeare of India," contributed to Sanskrit literature with timeless works like "Shakuntala" and "Meghaduta," showcasing the language's expressive and poetic capabilities.

Sanskrit was not confined to the realms of religion and literature; it played a crucial role in scientific and mathematical treatises. Aryabhata's "Aryabhatiya," an influential astronomical work composed in the 5th century, exemplifies the use of Sanskrit as a scientific language. The treatise presented mathematical innovations, including the concept of zero, and contributed to the understanding of astronomy in ancient India.

The influence of Sanskrit expanded beyond the Indian subcontinent. The spread of Indian culture through trade and diplomatic relations led to the dissemination of Sanskrit texts to Southeast Asia and beyond. This cultural diffusion contributed to the adoption of Sanskrit as a language of learning and administration in various regions, leaving enduring imprints on local languages and cultures.

The decline of Sanskrit as a spoken language occurred over centuries, influenced by historical, political, and social changes. However, its status as a classical language endured. Sanskrit continued to be used for scholarly and religious purposes, and its grammarian tradition remained vibrant. The establishment of centers of learning, like the renowned universities of Nalanda and Vikramashila, contributed to the preservation and perpetuation of Sanskrit knowledge.

The colonial era witnessed both challenges and renewed interest in Sanskrit. British policies aimed at replacing Sanskrit with English as the medium of education posed a threat to its vitality. Yet, the translation of Sanskrit texts into European languages during this period kindled a global fascination with Indian philosophy, literature, and linguistics.

In independent India, efforts were made to revive and promote Sanskrit. The establishment of institutions dedicated to Sanskrit studies, like the Rashtriya Sanskrit Sansthan, aimed at preserving and propagating the language. Sanskrit remains a vibrant academic discipline, attracting scholars and students globally.

The development of Sanskrit as a classical language is a journey marked by linguistic refinement, philosophical profundity, and literary excellence. From its roots in the Vedic hymns to its zenith in classical literature and scholarly treatises, Sanskrit has been a vehicle for the transmission of knowledge, culture, and wisdom. Its legacy endures not only in academia but also in the cultural and spiritual heritage of India, underscoring the timeless contributions of this classical language to human civilization.

- Epics like Ramayana and Mahabharata: Themes and moral lessons

The epics of Ramayana and Mahabharata, two cornerstone works of ancient Indian literature, are rich repositories of profound themes and moral lessons that have resonated across centuries. Both epics delve into intricate narratives, offering not only captivating stories but also profound insights into human nature, ethics, and the complexities of life. Exploring the themes and moral lessons embedded in these epics provides a deep understanding of the cultural and philosophical underpinnings of ancient India.

Themes of Ramayana:

1. Dharma (Righteous Duty):

- The Ramayana, attributed to the sage Valmiki, revolves around the concept of dharma. Rama, the protagonist, exemplifies unwavering adherence to his dharma as a prince, son, husband, and eventually, as a king.

- The epic emphasizes the importance of fulfilling one's duty with integrity, even in the face of personal sacrifices.

2. Ideal Leadership:

- The character of Rama embodies the qualities of an ideal leader. His commitment to justice, compassion, and the welfare of his subjects sets a standard for righteous governance.

- The narrative underscores the responsibilities and challenges of leadership, portraying Rama as a selfless and just ruler.

3. Loyalty and Devotion:

- The bond between Rama and his devoted wife, Sita, symbolizes loyalty and unwavering devotion. Sita's steadfastness during her trials and Rama's relentless pursuit to rescue her exemplify the strength of marital commitment.

- Hanuman's devotion to Rama, as portrayed in the Sundara Kanda, further underscores the theme of unwavering loyalty.

4. Consequences of Actions:

- The Ramayana explores the consequences of actions and decisions. Rama's exile, Sita's abduction, and the eventual war with Ravana illustrate the ripple effects of individual choices.

- The concept of karma, the law of cause and effect, is interwoven into the narrative, emphasizing that every action has repercussions.

5. Triumph of Good over Evil:

- The central conflict between Rama and the demon king Ravana represents the eternal struggle between good and evil.

- Rama's victory over Ravana signifies the ultimate triumph of righteousness, reinforcing the belief that virtue prevails in the face of adversity.

Moral Lessons of Ramayana:

1. Integrity in Relationships:

- The Ramayana underscores the importance of integrity in relationships. Rama's unwavering commitment to dharma, even at personal cost, serves as a moral lesson in upholding principles within familial and societal bonds.

2. Duty and Sacrifice:

- Rama's willingness to sacrifice personal happiness for the greater good exemplifies the concept of duty and sacrifice.

- The epic imparts the lesson that individuals must prioritize their responsibilities and commitments over personal desires.

3. Respect for Women:

- The narrative addresses the issue of female honor and respect. Sita's purity and virtue become symbolic, and Rama's unwavering commitment to her vindicates the significance of respecting and protecting women.

4. Humility and Devotion:

- Characters like Hanuman embody humility and unwavering devotion. Hanuman's selfless service to Rama, showcasing humility despite his extraordinary abilities, serves as a lesson in devotion and humility.

5. Ethical Leadership:

- The Ramayana extols the virtues of ethical leadership. Rama's adherence to dharma as a ruler sets an example for leaders to prioritize justice, compassion, and the welfare of their subjects.

Themes of Mahabharata:

1. Dharma and Adharma:

- The Mahabharata, attributed to the sage Vyasa, revolves around the concept of dharma and adharma, righteousness and unrighteousness.

- The Kurukshetra War, the epic's central conflict, emerges from a complex web of familial, societal, and political dharma.

2. Duty and Responsibility:

- The characters in the Mahabharata grapple with their duties and responsibilities. Arjuna's moral dilemma on the battlefield reflects the broader theme of navigating conflicting duties and responsibilities.

3. Complexities of Human Relationships:

- The Mahabharata delves into the complexities of human relationships, especially within the Kuru dynasty. The rivalry between the Pandavas and Kauravas, Draupadi's plight, and the intricate family dynamics illustrate the challenges inherent in relationships.

4. Power and Governance:

- The epic explores the complexities of power and governance. The struggle for Hastinapura's throne, the implications of unbridled ambition, and the consequences of flawed governance offer profound insights into political and ethical dilemmas.

5. The Nature of Existence:

- The Mahabharata delves into philosophical inquiries about the nature of existence, mortality, and the eternal cosmic order. Dialogues like the Bhagavad Gita, embedded within the epic, provide profound reflections on life, duty, and spirituality.

Moral Lessons of Mahabharata:

1. Ethical Decision-Making:

- The Mahabharata emphasizes the importance of ethical decision-making. Arjuna's moral struggle on the battlefield prompts a discourse on righteous action and the consequences of moral choices.

2. Consequences of Attachment:

- The narrative illustrates the consequences of attachment and desire. The Kauravas' unquenchable thirst for power and the Pandavas' attachment to their kingdom contribute to the unfolding tragedy.

3. Importance of Forgiveness:

- Forgiveness emerges as a prominent moral lesson. The reconciliation between the Pandavas and Kauravas in the aftermath of the war highlights the transformative power of forgiveness in resolving conflicts.

4. Role of Women:

- The Mahabharata presents nuanced portrayals of women, with characters like Draupadi and Kunti displaying resilience and strength in the face of adversity.

- Draupadi's dignified response to humiliation and her eventual forgiveness convey lessons of fortitude and compassion.

5. Spiritual Wisdom:

- The Bhagavad Gita, a key component of the Mahabharata, imparts spiritual wisdom. Lord Krishna's teachings to Arjuna transcend the battlefield, offering insights into duty, righteousness, and the path to spiritual enlightenment.

- Classical works of poetry, drama, and philosophy

Ancient India, with its rich cultural and intellectual heritage, produced classical works of poetry, drama, and philosophy that have left an indelible mark on the world. From the sublime verses of Kalidasa to the philosophical depth of texts like the Upanishads, these classical works exemplify the intellectual prowess and cultural vibrancy of ancient Indian civilization.

Poetry:

1. Kalidasa's "Shakuntala" and "Meghaduta":

- **"Shakuntala":** Kalidasa's "Shakuntala" stands as a pinnacle of Sanskrit drama. The narrative weaves a tale of love, separation, and reunion, focusing on the virtuous Shakuntala and her union with King Dushyanta. The play explores themes of love, morality, and the consequences of forgetting one's duty.

- **"Meghaduta":** In "Meghaduta," Kalidasa takes a different poetic route, crafting a lyrical masterpiece where a cloud messenger conveys the pining of a separated lover to his beloved. The poem is a celebration of nature's beauty, love, and the yearning for reunion.

2. Bhasa's Plays:

- Bhasa, a renowned ancient Indian playwright, contributed significantly to Sanskrit drama. Though most of his works are lost, some fragments and adaptations remain. His plays, like "Swapnavasavadatta" and "Madhyamavyayoga," are known for their dramatic intensity and exploration of complex human emotions.

3. Sanskrit Anthologies:

- Anthologies like the "Panchatantra" and "Sanskrit Subhashitas" represent the diverse expressions of ancient Indian poetry. The "Panchatantra," attributed to Vishnu Sharma, is a collection of moral stories narrated through animal fables, imparting wisdom and ethical lessons.

4. Tamil Sangam Poetry:

- The classical Tamil Sangam poetry, composed in various anthologies like the "Akananuru" and "Purananuru," provides insights into the cultural and social milieu of ancient South India. Themes of love, war, and nature dominate these poems, showcasing the linguistic and literary brilliance of Tamil poets.

Drama:

1. Sanskrit Dramas:

- Besides Kalidasa and Bhasa, Sanskrit dramas by playwrights like Sudraka ("Mrichakatika") and Bhavabhuti ("Uttararamacarita") have made significant contributions. These works delve into intricate plots, moral dilemmas, and the complexities of human relationships.

2. Natyashastra:

- The "Natyashastra," attributed to the sage Bharata, is a seminal treatise on dramaturgy and the performing arts. This ancient text comprehensively explores the principles of staging a drama, including aspects of plot, character, emotion, and aesthetics. It serves as a foundational guide for classical Indian performing arts.

3. Bhavabhuti's "Uttararamacarita":

- Bhavabhuti's "Uttararamacarita" is a Sanskrit drama that continues the narrative of the Ramayana. It focuses on the later life of Rama and his confrontation with his sons. The play delves into themes of duty, sacrifice, and the challenges faced by rulers.

4. Tamil Silappadikaram:

- "Silappadikaram," attributed to the poet Ilango Adigal, is a classical Tamil epic that weaves a tale of love, betrayal, and redemption. The narrative unfolds against the backdrop of the ancient Tamil city of Puhar and provides insights into the cultural and social life of the time.

Philosophy:

1. Upanishads:

- The Upanishads, a collection of philosophical texts, explore the nature of reality, the self (Atman), and the ultimate reality (Brahman). The dialogues in these texts between teachers and students delve into profound metaphysical and ethical inquiries.

2. Nyaya and Vaisheshika Sutras:

- The Nyaya and Vaisheshika Sutras are foundational texts in Indian philosophy. The Nyaya Sutras, attributed to sage Gautama, systematically explore logic and epistemology. The Vaisheshika Sutras, attributed to sage Kanada, delve into atomistic metaphysics and the nature of the physical world.

3. Samkhya Karika:

- The "Samkhya Karika," attributed to Sage Kapila, is a foundational text in Samkhya philosophy. It outlines the principles of this dualistic school of thought, emphasizing the distinction between the eternal and unchanging Purusha (consciousness) and Prakriti (matter).

4. Yoga Sutras of Patanjali:

- Attributed to the sage Patanjali, the "Yoga Sutras" provide a systematic guide to the practice of yoga. The text outlines the eight limbs of yoga, including ethical principles (yamas and niyamas), physical postures (asanas), breath control (pranayama), and meditation.

5. Advaita Vedanta:

- Shankaracharya's commentaries on the Upanishads, Bhagavad Gita, and Brahma Sutras form the basis of Advaita Vedanta. This non-dualistic philosophy asserts the identity of the individual soul (Atman) with the ultimate reality (Brahman) and emphasizes self-realization as the path to liberation (moksha).

6. Mimamsa Sutras:

- Jaimini's "Mimamsa Sutras" explore the principles of Mimamsa, a school of thought focused on ritual interpretation and the philosophy of language. The text delves into the interpretation of Vedic rituals and the nature of linguistic meaning.

7. Arthashastra:

- Attributed to Chanakya (Kautilya), the "Arthashastra" is an ancient treatise on statecraft, politics, and economics. It provides insights into governance, diplomacy, and the ethical conduct of rulers, offering a comprehensive guide to the administrationof a state. The text covers various aspects, including law, taxation, military strategy, and the responsibilities of the ruler.

Cultural Synthesis:

- These classical works exemplify the synthesis of diverse cultural influences within the Indian subcontinent. The Sanskrit dramas draw from regional traditions, and the Tamil Sangam poetry reflects the linguistic and cultural richness of South India. This cultural synthesis contributed to the unity in diversity that characterizes Indian civilization.

Universal Themes:

- The themes explored in these classical works transcend cultural and temporal boundaries. Love, duty, morality, and the search for ultimate truth are universal concerns that resonate across different societies and ages. The timeless nature of these themes contributes to the enduring relevance of these classical works.

Holistic Exploration:

- Collectively, these works offer a holistic exploration of human existence. Poetry delves into the realm of emotions, drama explores the complexities of relationships, and philosophy delves into the nature of reality and the self. This multidimensional approach reflects the richness of the human experience.

Philosophical Foundations:

- The philosophical texts, from the Upanishads to the Yoga Sutras, laid the foundations for various schools of thought, influencing not only Indian philosophy but also contributing to global philosophical discourse. The profound inquiries into the nature of consciousness, reality, and ethical conduct continue to inspire scholars worldwide.

Practical Guidance:

- Texts like the Arthashastra provide practical guidance for governance, reflecting the practical wisdom embedded in ancient Indian thought. The emphasis on ethical leadership, the welfare of the state, and the responsibilities of rulers underscores the integration of ethics with political and economic considerations.

Legacy and Contemporary Relevance:

- The legacy of these classical works is evident in the continuity of cultural practices, philosophical traditions, and artistic expressions in contemporary India. The principles outlined in these texts continue to influence various aspects of life, from literature to governance to the practice of yoga.

Challenges and Continuity:

- While these classical works have endured, their preservation faced challenges over the centuries. Manuscripts were at risk of deterioration, and the oral transmission of some texts faced threats of extinction. However, the dedicated efforts of scholars, institutions, and modern technologies have contributed to their preservation and dissemination.

Revitalization Efforts:

- In independent India, there have been concerted efforts to revitalize the study and appreciation of classical literature and philosophy. Academic institutions, research centers, and cultural organizations play a crucial role in preserving, translating, and interpreting these texts for contemporary audiences.

Global Influence:

- The global interest in Indian philosophy, literature, and arts, fueled by translations and academic engagement, demonstrates the enduring influence of classical Indian works beyond national borders. Yoga, inspired by ancient philosophical and spiritual traditions, has become a global phenomenon, showcasing the international impact of these classical teachings.

The classical works of poetry, drama, and philosophy from ancient India represent a treasure trove of human wisdom, creativity, and philosophical insights. From the sublime verses of Kalidasa to the profound inquiries of the Upanishads, these texts continue to inspire and enrich the cultural and intellectual landscape, bridging the past with the present and transcending cultural boundaries. Their legacy endures as a testament to the intellectual brilliance and cultural diversity of ancient India. The classical works of poetry, drama, and philosophy from ancient India form a profound tapestry of intellectual and cultural achievements. From the lyrical verses of Kalidasa to the philosophical inquiries of the Upanishads, these texts reflect the diverse expressions of human thought, creativity, and spirituality.

Chapter 8:

Music, Dance and Theatre

Ancient India's cultural tapestry is adorned with vibrant expressions of music, dance, and theatre, reflecting a harmonious blend of spirituality and artistic creativity. Classical Indian music, rooted in ragas and talas, embodies a deep spiritual connection, with instruments like the sitar and tabla weaving intricate melodies.

Classical dance forms, such as Bharatanatyam, Kathak, Odissi, and Kuchipudi, are a visual feast of graceful movements and expressive storytelling. These dances often draw inspiration from ancient texts and mythologies, becoming a dynamic medium for cultural preservation.

Theatre, as seen in Sanskrit dramas and folk traditions, captivated audiences with compelling narratives. Natyashastra, a foundational treatise on performing arts, laid the groundwork for intricate theatrical productions, blending music, dance, and drama seamlessly. Collectively, these artistic expressions reflect the deep spiritual and cultural ethos that continues to resonate in contemporary India's diverse performing arts landscape.

- Role of music and dance in ancient Indian society

In ancient Indian society, music and dance were integral components that transcended mere entertainment, playing profound roles in religious, social, and cultural spheres. Rooted in spirituality and expressing the essence of Indian philosophy, these art forms were not just aesthetic expressions but gateways to transcendence.

Religious Significance:

Music and dance were deeply intertwined with religious practices. The Vedas, ancient sacred texts, emphasized the spiritual power of sound, leading to the development of sacred chants and hymns. The Samaveda, specifically dedicated to musical notation, highlighted the importance of melodic intonations in rituals. Music, as a devotional offering, was a means of connecting with the divine, fostering a spiritual atmosphere during religious ceremonies.

Dance, too, had a sacred dimension. Temples served as hubs for artistic expression, and intricate dance forms were dedicated to specific deities. Bharatanatyam, for instance, originated in temples, with intricate hand gestures and rhythmic footwork telling mythological stories. The dance itself was considered an offering to the divine, embodying the union of body, mind, and soul.

Cultural and Social Functions:

In the social realm, music and dance played crucial roles in community cohesion and celebration. Festivals, weddings, and other communal events were marked by vibrant performances. Folk dances like Garba and Bihu celebrated regional diversity, fostering a sense of unity.

The Natyashastra, attributed to the sage Bharata, served as a comprehensive guide to the performing arts. It delineated the aesthetics of dance, music, and drama, providing a structured framework for artistic expression. This ancient treatise emphasized the moral and ethical responsibilities of artists, highlighting the cultural and social impact of these art forms.

Educational Significance:

Education in ancient India was not confined to textbooks; it extended to the arts. The Gurukul system, where students lived with their teachers, included training in music and dance. Students imbibed values, discipline, and cultural awareness through these art forms, fostering a holistic educational experience.

Music and dance were considered essential components of a well-rounded education, promoting creativity, emotional expression, and physical discipline. The Natyashastra recognized the educational value of the performing arts, incorporating them into the curriculum to nurture a balanced and culturally enriched individual.

Healing and Meditation:

The therapeutic aspects of music were well understood in ancient India. The Gandharva Veda, a branch of knowledge related to music, addressed the healing properties of specific ragas and rhythms. Ragas were believed to have specific effects on the body and mind, contributing to physical and mental well-being. Dance, too, had meditative qualities. The precise movements and postures in classical dance forms were not just artistic expressions but also served as a form of meditation. The alignment of body, breath, and rhythm facilitated a meditative state, promoting mental focus and emotional balance.

Expressing Emotions and Narratives:

Music and dance were powerful tools for expressing a range of human emotions. Raga and tala, the foundational elements of Indian music, were crafted to evoke specific emotions. Compositions explored the nuances of joy, sorrow, love, and devotion, providing a nuanced language to articulate human experience. Dance, with its intricate mudras (hand gestures) and abhinaya (expressions), conveyed narratives with profound emotional depth. Dancers became storytellers, embodying characters from epics and myths, making the art form a repository of cultural narratives.

Influence on Other Art Forms:

Music and dance were not isolated; they influenced other art forms like poetry and sculpture. Poetic meters were often linked to specific musical rhythms, creating a rhythmic symmetry. Sculptures in temples often depicted dancers and musicians, immortalizing these art forms as integral components of cultural expression.

Challenges and Preservation:

Despite their significance, these art forms faced challenges. The decline of royal patronage and the socio-economic shifts during various periods posed threats to the survival of classical arts. However, dedicated practitioners and the oral tradition played a crucial role in preserving and transmitting these art forms through generations.

Contemporary Relevance:

Today, classical music and dance continue to thrive, adapting to modern contexts while maintaining their traditional essence. Institutions, festivals, and educational programs contribute to their preservation. Moreover, the global appreciation of Indian classical arts underscores their universal appeal, demonstrating that the ancient roles of music and dance remain relevant in the contemporary world.

In essence, the roles of music and dance in ancient Indian society were multifaceted. Beyond entertainment, they were pathways to the divine, agents of social cohesion, tools for education and healing, and mediums for emotional expression. The legacy of these art forms endures, bridging the past with the present and enriching the cultural fabric of India.

- The Natya Shastra and the theory of performing arts

The Natya Shastra, attributed to the ancient sage Bharata, stands as a seminal treatise that comprehensively explores the theory and practice of performing arts. This foundational text, believed to have been composed between the 2nd century BCE and 2nd century CE, not only laid the groundwork for Indian classical dance, music, and drama but also provided a holistic framework for understanding the aesthetics and philosophy of the performing arts.

Components of the Natya Shastra:

1. Classification of Arts:

Bharata categorizes the arts into two main types: the fine arts (shastriya) and the folk or traditional arts (lokika). The Natya Shastra primarily focuses on the shastriya, which includes classical music, dance, and drama.

2. Origin of Natya:

According to Bharata, the origin of Natya (drama) is divine. He describes the creation of drama by Lord Brahma and emphasizes its purpose as both entertainment and edification.

3. Rasa Theory:

Central to the Natya Shastra is the concept of Rasa, the aesthetic essence or flavor evoked in the audience. Bharata identifies eight primary Rasas: Shringara (love), Hasya (laughter), Karuna (compassion), Raudra (anger), Veera (heroic), Bhayanaka (fear), Bibhatsa (disgust), and Adbhuta (wonder). Each Rasa corresponds to a specific emotion and is experienced through the convergence of various artistic elements.

4. Elements of Drama (Natyadharmi and Lokadharmi):

The text distinguishes between Natyadharmi (conventional or stylized representation) and Lokadharmi (realistic representation). Natyadharmi includes the specific rules and conventions of the performing arts, while Lokadharmi encompasses naturalistic and everyday expressions.

5. Bhavas and Vibhavas:

Bharata identifies Bhavas as the fundamental emotional states that actors must convey to evoke Rasa. These Bhavas are complemented by Vibhavas (determinants) and Anubhavas (consequents), collectively creating a nuanced emotional landscape in a performance.

6. Angika, Vachika, Sattvika, and Aharya Abhinaya:

Bharata categorizes expressions into Angika (body movements), Vachika (verbal expressions), Sattvika (internal emotions), and Aharya (costumes and makeup) Abhinaya. These elements, when harmoniously integrated, result in a comprehensive portrayal of characters and emotions.

7. Music and Dance in Natya:

The Natya Shastra provides detailed insights into the use of music and dance in drama. It classifies musical notes, describes various musical instruments, and outlines the different types of dances. The coordination of music and dance is considered essential for a successful performance.

8. Rasa Dhvani:

Bharata introduces the concept of Rasa Dhvani, the power of suggestion. He suggests that the primary aim of poetry and drama is to create emotional resonance, and this resonance is achieved through the evocation of Rasa.

9. Theater Design and Architecture:

Natya Shastra also delves into the design and construction of theaters. It outlines the ideal dimensions, the placement of the audience, and the importance of a stage conducive to effective performance.

10. Acting Techniques:

Detailed instructions are provided for actors, including guidance on expression, postures, and the modulation of voice. The text emphasizes the need for actors to understand the psychological aspects of their characters to deliver authentic performances.

Legacy and Impact:

1. Preservation of Tradition:

The Natya Shastra has played a crucial role in preserving and codifying classical performing arts traditions. Its principles have been passed down through generations, contributing to the continuity of Indian classical dance and drama.

2. Influence on Regional Traditions:

While the Natya Shastra served as a foundational text for Indian classical arts, it also influenced regional performance traditions. Different styles of classical dance and theater across India draw inspiration from Bharata's principles.

3. Global Recognition:

The Natya Shastra has garnered attention and respect globally as a comprehensive treatise on the theory of performing arts. Its principles continue to be studied and appreciated by scholars and practitioners worldwide.

4. Adaptation and Evolution:

The principles laid down in the Natya Shastra have provided a solid foundation for the evolution of performing arts. Contemporary artists, while respecting the classical traditions, continue to innovate and adapt, ensuring the relevance of Bharata's insights in a modern context.

The Natya Shastra stands as a monumental work that encapsulates the theoretical framework of Indian classical performing arts. Its enduring legacy lies not only in its historical significance but also in its continued influence on the practice and understanding of the rich tapestry of Indian performing arts.

- Regional variations in music and dance forms

India, with its diverse cultural landscape, is a mosaic of regional variations in music and dance forms. The rich tapestry of these artistic expressions reflects the historical, social, and geographical nuances of each region. From the classical traditions rooted in ancient texts to the vibrant folk forms passed down through generations, the regional diversity of Indian music and dance is a testament to the country's cultural richness.

North India:

1. Classical Music:

- **Hindustani Classical Music:** Predominant in North India, Hindustani classical music has evolved from the ancient traditions outlined in texts like the Natya Shastra. It is characterized by its emphasis on improvisation, intricate ragas, and talas. Instruments such as the sitar, tabla, and sarod are integral to this tradition.

2. Classical Dance:

- **Kathak:** Originating in North India, Kathak is a classical dance form known for its intricate footwork and graceful expressions. It often incorporates storytelling through rhythmic patterns and facial expressions.

3. Folk Music and Dance:

- **Bhangra and Giddha:** Originating in Punjab, Bhangra is a lively dance form accompanied by vibrant music, often celebrating harvest or festivals. Giddha is a traditional dance performed by women, characterized by graceful movements and lively gestures.

- **Rasiya:** From the Braj region, Rasiya is a form of folk music and dance that narrates tales of Lord Krishna. It involves colorful costumes, expressive dance, and traditional musical instruments.

South India:

1. Classical Music:

- **Carnatic Classical Music:** Predominant in South India, Carnatic music is rooted in ancient Sanskrit texts. It places a strong emphasis on precise rendering of ragas and talas. Instruments like the veena, mridangam, and violin are commonly used.

2. Classical Dance:

- **Bharatanatyam:** Originating in Tamil Nadu, Bharatanatyam is one of the oldest classical dance forms in India. It combines intricate footwork, expressive gestures, and storytelling. The dance often portrays mythological narratives.

3. Folk Music and Dance:

- **Kuchipudi:** Hailing from Andhra Pradesh, Kuchipudi is a classical dance form that incorporates both masculine and feminine elements. It often narrates stories from Hindu mythology through expressive movements and elaborate costumes.

- **Yakshagana:** Found in Karnataka, Yakshagana is a traditional theater form that combines dance, music, and dialogue. It often depicts stories from the epics and involves vibrant makeup and costumes.

East India:

1. Classical Music:

- **Odissi Classical Music:** Rooted in the ancient Odia

traditions, Odissi music accompanies the classical dance form of Odissi. The music is characterized by lyrical compositions and rhythmic patterns.

2. Classical Dance:

- **Odissi:** Originating in Odisha, Odissi is a classical dance form known for its fluid movements, intricate postures, and storytelling. It often depicts episodes from the epics and incorporates sculpturesque poses.

3. Folk Music and Dance:

- **Bihu:** Celebrated in Assam, Bihu is an energetic folk dance accompanied by traditional music. It is performed during the Bihu festival and reflects the vibrancy of Assamese culture.

- **Chhau:** Spread across West Bengal, Jharkhand, and Odisha, Chhau is a traditional dance form that combines martial arts, acrobatics, and storytelling. Performers wear elaborate masks and costumes.

West India:

1. Classical Music:

- **Gujarati Classical Music:** Rooted in the rich cultural heritage of Gujarat, classical music in this region often reflects the devotional and folk traditions. Instruments like the flute, tabla, and harmonium are commonly used.

2. Classical Dance:

- **Kathak:** While Kathak originated in North India, it has influences in West India as well. The expressive dance form is characterized by intricate footwork, fast spins, and storytelling.

3. Folk Music and Dance:

- **Garba and Raas:** Predominant in Gujarat, Garba and Raas are traditional dance forms performed during festivals like Navratri. They involve circular movements, rhythmic clapping, and vibrant costumes.

- **Tamasha:** Found in Maharashtra, Tamasha is a traditional folk theater form that combines music, dance, and drama. It often portrays social issues through lively performances.

Central India:

1. Classical Music:

- **Malwa Classical Music:** Reflecting the cultural heritage of the Malwa region in Madhya Pradesh, classical music in this area often incorporates folk elements. The use of traditional instruments and melodic compositions is prominent.

2. Folk Music and Dance:

- **Matki Dance:** Popular in Rajasthan and parts of Madhya Pradesh, Matki Dance involves women balancing earthen pots on their heads while dancing. It is a lively and colorful folk dance performed during festivals.

North-East India:

1. Folk Music and Dance:

- **Nongkrem Dance:** Celebrated by the Khasi tribe in

Meghalaya, Nongkrem Dance is performed during the annual Nongkrem Festival. It involves rhythmic steps and traditional music, providing a glimpse into the cultural practices of the region.

Islands of India:

1. Folk Music and Dance:

- **Lavani:** Originating in Maharashtra, Lavani is a traditional dance form known for its vibrant and energetic movements. It is often performed to the accompaniment of Lavani music, which includes rhythmic beats and expressive lyrics.

Cross-Regional Influences:

- Over centuries, India has witnessed cross-regional influences where artists from one part of the country have enriched the cultural heritage of another. This exchange has contributed to the diversity and dynamism of Indian music and dance.

Contemporary Trends:

- In contemporary times, artists often blend traditional forms with modern influences, creating innovative and fusion performances. This dynamic evolution ensures the continued relevance and appeal of Indian music and dance on the global stage.

The regional variations in music and dance forms across India showcase the country's cultural kaleidoscope. Each region's unique traditions, influenced by history, geography, and societal practices, contribute to the vibrant and diverse tapestry of Indian performing arts. These artistic expressions not only reflect the rich heritage of India but also continue to evolve, ensuring their enduring relevance in the cultural

Chapter 9

Science, Mathematics and Technology

Ancient India made significant contributions to science, mathematics, and technology. In mathematics, the concept of zero and the decimal system originated, laying the foundation for modern arithmetic. Aryabhata's astronomical work and the development of trigonometry showcased advanced mathematical knowledge. In science, Ayurveda, an ancient medical system, flourished, emphasizing holistic well-being. The Iron Pillar of Delhi stands as a testament to advanced metallurgical skills. India's ancient achievements continue to influence contemporary knowledge, highlighting a rich legacy in science, mathematics, and technology that resonates through the ages.

- Contributions of ancient Indians in mathematics (numerals, zero), astronomy, and medicine

Ancient India stands as a beacon of intellectual prowess, making profound contributions to mathematics, astronomy, and medicine. The legacy of Indian scholars reverberates through the annals of history, shaping the foundations of these disciplines and influencing global knowledge.

Mathematics: Numerals and Zero

1. Decimal System:

The revolutionary Indian numeral system, also known as the decimal system, forms the cornerstone of modern arithmetic. The use of zero and a place-value system allowed for efficient representation of numbers. This system, documented in the works of mathematicians like Brahmagupta, laid the groundwork for the numerical notations used worldwide today.

2. Zero:

The concept of zero, a fundamental mathematical concept, found explicit representation in ancient Indian texts. The mathematician Brahmagupta, in his seminal work "Brahmasphutasiddhanta," provided rules for arithmetic operations involving zero. The Indian mathematician Pingala introduced binary numbers in the "Chhandahshastra," influencing future developments in computer science.

3. Aryabhata's Contributions:

Aryabhata, a prominent mathematician and astronomer, made groundbreaking contributions to algebra and trigonometry. His work, "Aryabhatiya," introduced algorithms for solving linear and quadratic equations. Aryabhata's sine table, an early version of trigonometric functions, showcased the advanced mathematical knowledge of ancient Indians.

Astronomy: Advancements in Celestial Knowledge

1. Aryabhata's Astronomical Treatise:

Aryabhata's contributions extended to astronomy, where his work "Aryabhatiya" provided insights into celestial movements. He accurately calculated the length of a solar year, emphasizing the Earth's rotation on its axis. Aryabhata's heliocentric model anticipated Copernicus' later formulation by centuries.

2. Surya Siddhanta:

The "Surya Siddhanta," an ancient Sanskrit text on astronomy, offered precise methods for calculating planetary positions and eclipses. It introduced trigonometric concepts and provided a detailed understanding of celestial phenomena. While its exact origins are uncertain, it significantly influenced Indian and Greek astronomical thought.

3. Varahamihira's Contributions:

Varahamihira, a polymath of the 6th century, made notable contributions to astronomy in his work "Panchasiddhantika." He integrated ideas from various astronomical traditions and compiled five astronomical systems. His accurate predictions of celestial events demonstrated a sophisticated understanding of planetary motion.

Medicine: Ayurveda and Holistic Healthcare

1. Ayurveda:

Ancient India gave birth to Ayurveda, a holistic system of medicine that has endured for millennia. The foundational Ayurvedic texts, including the "Charaka Samhita" and the "Sushruta Samhita," outlined principles of healthcare, surgery, and herbal medicine. Ayurveda emphasizes the balance of bodily humors and individualized approaches to well-being.

2. Sushruta's Surgical Expertise:

Sushruta, often hailed as the father of surgery, made remarkable contributions to the field. The "Suṣhruta Samhita" detailed surgical procedures, including plastic surgery and cataract operations. Sushruta's understanding of anatomy and surgical techniques was highly advanced for its time.

3. Contributions to Pharmacology:

Ancient Indians excelled in pharmacology, as evident in texts like the "Charaka Samhita." Herbal remedies, minerals, and metals were meticulously documented for their medicinal properties. Ayurvedic pharmacology recognized the interconnectedness of the body and the environment, emphasizing personalized treatments.

Legacy and Global Impact

1. Transmission of Knowledge:

Ancient Indian mathematical, astronomical, and medical knowledge spread beyond the Indian subcontinent through trade and cultural exchanges. Arab scholars played a crucial role in translating and disseminating these texts, preserving and transmitting Indian intellectual achievements to the Islamic world and, eventually, Europe.

2. Influence on Islamic Scholars:

The works of Indian mathematicians and astronomers deeply influenced Islamic scholars during the Golden Age of Islamic civilization. Al-Khwarizmi, a Persian mathematician, integrated Indian numeral and algebraic concepts into his works, laying the foundation for modern algebra.

3. Continued Relevance:

The contributions of ancient Indians in mathematics, astronomy, and medicine continue to be relevant. The Indian numeral system, including zero, is universally adopted, facilitating complex mathematical calculations. Ayurveda's holistic approach has inspired integrative medicine, emphasizing the interconnectedness of physical, mental, and spiritual well-being.

Challenges and Preservation

1. Manuscript Tradition:

The preservation of ancient Indian knowledge faced challenges, particularly during periods of political upheaval. Manuscripts were vulnerable to decay and destruction, yet dedicated efforts by scholars and institutions helped preserve these texts.

2. Rediscovery and Recognition:

The rediscovery of ancient Indian mathematical and scientific achievements occurred during the colonial era. European scholars recognized the depth of Indian contributions, challenging earlier Eurocentric narratives.

3. Modern Revival:

In independent India, there has been a resurgence of interest in reviving and studying ancient knowledge systems. Institutions like the Indian National Science Academy actively promote the exploration of historical contributions to science and mathematics.

Ancient India's contributions in mathematics, astronomy, and medicine exemplify a profound intellectual heritage. The Indian numeral system, the concept of zero, astronomical models, surgical techniques, and Ayurvedic principles collectively form a legacy that transcends time and borders. These contributions not only shaped the historical narrative but also continue to resonate in contemporary global scientific and medical discourses. The enduring impact of ancient Indian scholars underscores the richness of India's intellectual tapestry and its enduring relevance in the broader context of human knowledge.

- Technological advancements: Metallurgy, shipbuilding, textiles

Ancient India witnessed remarkable technological advancements in metallurgy, shipbuilding, and textiles, contributing to its economic prosperity and cultural exchange.

Metallurgy:

1. Iron and Steel Production:

- The Iron Pillar of Delhi, dating back to the 4th century CE, stands as a testament to advanced metallurgical skills. Its corrosion resistance showcases a high level of iron mastery.

- Wootz steel, produced in ancient India, was renowned for its quality. The knowledge of crucible steel-making spread to the Middle East and played a significant role in the development of Damascus steel.

2. Metal Alloys:

- Bronze casting was prevalent in the Indus Valley Civilization, indicating proficiency in alloying copper with tin. Bronze artifacts showcased not only aesthetic finesse but also technological expertise.

Shipbuilding:

1. Knowledge of Maritime Trade:

- The Harappans engaged in maritime trade with regions like Mesopotamia, indicating advanced shipbuilding skills. Dockyards discovered at Lothal highlight the planning and engineering involved in the construction of seafaring vessels.

2. Sewn Plank Technique:

- Ancient Indian shipbuilders used the sewn plank technique, stitching wooden planks together with coir ropes. This method, showcased in the construction of large ships, enhanced durability and flexibility.

3. Navigation Techniques:

- Ancient Indian sailors were adept at navigation, using the stars and celestial bodies for guidance. The treatise "Samudrika Shastra" provided insights into ship design, navigation, and even maritime weather predictions.

Textiles:

1. Cotton Cultivation:

- The knowledge of cotton cultivation and processing was widespread in ancient India. Cotton textiles from the Indus Valley Civilization, showcased in artifacts like the Mohenjo-Daro's "Great Bath" and the "Priest King" statue, attest to advanced textile production.

2. Dyeing Techniques:

- Ancient Indians were proficient in dyeing techniques. The use of vibrant natural dyes, such as indigo and madder, added intricate patterns and colors to textiles.

3. Muslin and Silk:

- The art of producing fine muslin fabric reached its pinnacle in ancient India. Dhaka in present-day Bangladesh was renowned for its muslin, prized for its delicacy.

- Sericulture, the cultivation of silk, thrived in various regions. The silk trade flourished along the Silk Road, connecting India to the wider world.

Legacy and Impact:

1. Cultural Exchange:

- The proficiency in shipbuilding facilitated cultural exchange through maritime trade. Indian textiles, spices, and precious stones were sought after, influencing the global trade network.

2. Technological Diffusion:

- Technological knowledge in metallurgy, especially the production of high-quality steel, diffused to other parts of the world, influencing developments in weaponry and tools.

3. Economic Prosperity:

- Technological advancements in textiles, particularly the production of muslin and silk, contributed to economic prosperity. India's textiles were highly sought after in international markets.

Challenges and Preservation:

1. Loss of Techniques:

- Over time, certain ancient techniques in metallurgy, shipbuilding, and textiles were lost or declined, often due to changing socio-political dynamics and economic priorities.

2. Preservation Efforts:

- Archaeological excavations and studies play a crucial role in uncovering and preserving knowledge about ancient technologies. Preservation efforts include the documentation of archaeological sites, artifacts, and traditional practices.

The technological advancements in metallurgy, shipbuilding, and textiles in ancient India were not only indicators of technical prowess but also catalysts for cultural exchange and economic growth. These innovations, rooted in ancient wisdom, had a lasting impact on global trade and technological diffusion. The legacy of these advancements continues to be recognized, studied, and preserved, emphasizing the importance of ancient India's contributions to the technological tapestry of human history.

- Scientific outlook in ancient Indian culture

Ancient Indian culture harbored a profound scientific outlook that permeated various aspects of life, from philosophy and astronomy to medicine and mathematics. The roots of this scientific temperament can be traced back to the Vedic period and further developed through subsequent ages, leaving an indelible mark on the intellectual heritage of the Indian subcontinent.

Vedic Period: Pursuit of Knowledge

The Vedic texts, composed between 1500 BCE and 500 BCE, exemplify an inquisitive and contemplative approach towards the natural world. Rigveda, the oldest Veda, contains hymns that express admiration for the cosmic order and reflect a nascent scientific curiosity. The understanding of celestial bodies and their movements is evident in hymns dedicated to various deities associated with the cosmos.

Upanishads: Philosophical Inquiry and Cosmology

The Upanishads, emerging around 800 BCE, marked a shift

towards profound philosophical inquiries, laying the groundwork for a systematic exploration of reality. Concepts like "Brahman" (universal consciousness) and "Atman" (individual soul) were central to Upanishadic thought. The cosmological speculations within these texts hinted at a nuanced understanding of the interconnectedness of the universe.

Jainism and Buddhism: Empirical Observations

The sixth century BCE witnessed the emergence of Jainism and Buddhism, both emphasizing empirical observations and rational inquiry. Mahavira, the founder of Jainism, advocated a philosophy grounded in asceticism and non-violence. Gautama Buddha's teachings stressed the importance of mindfulness and understanding the nature of suffering. These philosophical traditions encouraged a rational approach to life's challenges.

Classical Period: Scientific Treatises

1. Astronomy: Aryabhata's Insights

Aryabhata, a prominent mathematician and astronomer from the Gupta period (5th century CE), authored the "Aryabhatiya." This treatise provided precise calculations for astronomical phenomena, including the length of a solar year and the Earth's rotation. Aryabhata's heliocentric model of the solar system demonstrated advanced astronomical thinking.

2. Medicine: Ayurveda's Holistic Approach

Ayurveda, an ancient system of medicine, emerged during the Vedic period and found systematic elaboration in texts like the "Charaka Samhita" and the "Sushruta Samhita." Ayurvedic practitioners recognized the interconnectedness of the body, mind, and spirit, prescribing holistic approaches to healthcare. The knowledge of medicinal herbs and surgical techniques showcased an empirical understanding of the human body.

3. Mathematics: The Concept of Zero

Indian mathematicians made pivotal contributions to the field. The concept of zero, crucial to mathematical notation, was developed in ancient India. Brahmagupta, in his work "Brahmasphutasiddhanta," laid down rules for arithmetic operations involving zero and negative numbers. The decimal numeral system, with positional notation, transformed mathematical representation.

Golden Age: Gupta Dynasty

The Gupta Dynasty (4th to 6th century CE) is often referred to as the Golden Age of Indian culture and science. During this period, scholars made significant strides in various disciplines, contributing to the flourishing intellectual environment.

1. Kalidasa's Observations on Nature

The renowned poet and playwright Kalidasa, through works like "Shakuntala" and "Meghaduta," demonstrated a keen observation of nature. His poetic descriptions reflected an appreciation for the environment, seasons, and celestial phenomena, underscoring a scientific awareness.

2. Varahamihira's Contributions

Varahamihira, a polymath of the Gupta era, authored the

"Panchasiddhantika," which synthesized five astronomical models. His work showcased a deep understanding of planetary motion and eclipses, contributing to the refinement of Indian astronomy.

Challenges and Preservation

The scientific outlook in ancient Indian culture faced challenges, including periods of political upheaval and the decline of certain knowledge systems. The preservation of scientific knowledge relied on the manuscript tradition, and dedicated efforts by scholars helped retain and transmit this knowledge across generations.

Continuity and Influence

The scientific outlook in ancient India had a lasting impact on subsequent intellectual developments. The transmission of Indian knowledge to the Islamic world, particularly during the Golden Age of Islamic civilization, facilitated a cross-cultural exchange that influenced European thought during the Renaissance.

Ancient Indian culture fostered a scientific outlook characterized by curiosity, empirical observations, and a profound appreciation for the interconnectedness of the natural world. From the Vedic period to the Gupta era, scholars in various fields contributed to a rich scientific heritage that continues to resonate. The pursuit of knowledge, as exemplified in astronomy, medicine, and mathematics, underscored an intellectual vibrancy that transcended temporal and geographical boundaries. The enduring legacy of the scientific temperament in ancient Indian culture is a testament to the timeless relevance of inquisitive inquiry and rational exploration.

Chapter 10

Social Structure and Daily Life

Ancient Indian society was structured hierarchically, shaped by the varna and jati system. At the top were the Brahmins (priests and scholars), followed by Kshatriyas (warriors and rulers), Vaishyas (merchants and farmers), and Shudras (laborers and servants). Beyond these varnas, there were numerous jatis, or subgroups, contributing to the complex social fabric.

Daily life varied based on one's position in this social structure. Brahmins performed religious rituals, Kshatriyas focused on governance and defense, Vaishyas engaged in trade and agriculture, while Shudras provided essential services. Rigidity in social roles was evident, yet common practices such as joint family living, reverence for elders, and adherence to dharma (righteous duty) formed the cultural foundation. The influence of religious texts like the Manusmriti and Dharmashastra further codified social norms, emphasizing duties and responsibilities within this intricate societal framework.

- Caste system and its evolution

The caste system in ancient India was a hierarchical social structure that classified people into distinct groups based on their occupation, birth, and social status. It evolved over centuries, and its origins can be traced to the Vedic period (1500 BCE to 500 BCE).

Vedic Period: Emergence of Varna System

The Vedic society initially had a simple division into four varnas (classes): Brahmins (priests and scholars), Kshatriyas (warriors and rulers), Vaishyas (merchants and farmers), and Shudras (laborers and servants). These varnas were initially based on one's natural inclination (guna) and occupation (karma).

Later Vedic Period: Rigidity and Hierarchical Ordering

As society progressed, the varna system became more rigid and hierarchical. The Manusmriti, a legal and ethical text dating back to around 200 BCE, played a significant role in codifying and reinforcing social hierarchies. It not only solidified the fourfold varna system but also introduced the concept of jatis (sub-castes) based on birth.

Post-Mauryan Period: Jati System and Specialization

Following the decline of the Mauryan Empire, the jati system gained prominence. Jatis became numerous, reflecting a more detailed and specialized division of labor. Individuals were now associated with specific hereditary occupations, further entrenching the social hierarchy.

Gupta Period: Consolidation of Caste Practices

The Gupta period (4th to 6th century CE) saw the consolidation of caste practices. Sanskrit texts like the Dharmashastra continued to uphold and legitimize the varna and jati system. Inter-caste marriages were discouraged, and social mobility was limited, perpetuating the inherited nature of one's social status.

Medieval Period: Influence of Islam

With the arrival of Islamic rulers in India, there was a degree of social mobility outside the caste system. However, the caste structure persisted in many regions, and the rigidity of social divisions remained a defining feature.

Colonial Period: Codification and Stigmatization

During British colonial rule, the census and legal systems contributed to the codification of caste identities. The British categorized communities into castes, inadvertently reinforcing existing social divisions. The stigmatization of certain castes, often based on occupational roles, deepened social inequalities.

Post-Independence: Constitutional Reforms

After India gained independence in 1947, efforts were made to address social inequalities. The Indian Constitution, adopted in 1950, outlawed untouchability and provided for affirmative action through reservations in education and jobs for historically marginalized communities, known as Scheduled Castes and Scheduled Tribes.

Contemporary India: Persistence and Challenges

While legal reforms aimed at addressing caste-based discrimination have made significant strides, social and economic disparities persist. The caste system's influence is still felt in various aspects of daily life, including marriage, social interactions, and political representation. Efforts to promote social justice and equality continue, but overcoming deeply ingrained social hierarchies remains a complex challenge.

The caste system in India evolved from an initial varna-based classification to a complex jati system, entwined with social, economic, and cultural facets. Its historical evolution reflects a combination of socio-religious practices, legal codifications, and external influences, contributing to the intricate tapestry of India's social structure.

- Analysis of the caste system and its impact on society, economy, and development.

Analysis of the Caste System and Its Impact on Society, Economy, and Development

1. Societal Impact:

- **Social Hierarchies:** The caste system perpetuated rigid social hierarchies, defining individuals' status and roles based on birth. This led to social divisions, discrimination, and limited opportunities for those in lower castes.

- **Endogamy and Social Isolation:** The system encouraged

endogamy, restricting marriages within one's caste. This practice reinforced social boundaries and led to the isolation of certain communities.

2. **Economic Impact:**

- **Occupational Restrictions:** Caste-based occupational roles limited individuals to specific professions, hindering economic mobility. Certain occupations were stigmatized, creating barriers to entrepreneurship and economic diversification.

- **Inequality in Wealth Distribution:** The caste system contributed to economic inequality, with certain castes having greater access to resources, education, and opportunities. This disparity persists, impacting economic development.

3. **Educational Impact:**

- **Limited Access to Education:** Historically, lower castes faced barriers to education, perpetuating a cycle of socio-economic disadvantage. Efforts to rectify this through affirmative action have made progress but challenges persist.

- **Educational Disparities:** Despite constitutional provisions for affirmative action, educational disparities continue, affecting the overall development of marginalized communities.

4. **Political Impact:**

- **Limited Political Representation:** Historically, certain castes were underrepresented in political spheres. While there have been improvements, challenges remain in achieving equitable political representation, impacting policy decisions.

5. Legal Reforms and Challenges:

- **Abolition of Untouchability:** Legal reforms, including the abolition of untouchability, aimed at addressing social discrimination. However, the effective implementation of these laws faces challenges at the grassroots level.

- **Affirmative Action:** Reservations for Scheduled Castes and Scheduled Tribes in education and employment have been implemented. While intended to address historical injustices, debates continue on the efficacy and unintended consequences of such policies.

6. Social Justice Movements:

- **Advocacy and Activism:** Social justice movements have emerged to challenge caste-based discrimination. Movements like the Dalit Panthers have sought to empower marginalized communities and raise awareness about social injustices.

7. Challenges in Modern India:

- **Urban-Rural Divide:** Caste dynamics persist in both urban and rural settings, contributing to an urban-rural divide. This divide can affect access to resources, services, and employment opportunities.

- **Changing Dynamics:** Globalization and urbanization have led to shifts in traditional caste dynamics. While some barriers have diminished, challenges related to social stigma and discrimination persist.

8. **Economic Development and Caste:**

- **Entrepreneurship and Economic Diversification:** Efforts to promote entrepreneurship and economic diversification among marginalized communities are crucial for overall economic development. Breaking occupational stereotypes is vital for creating a more inclusive economy.

- **Skill Development and Employment Opportunities:** Focused initiatives on skill development and providing equal employment opportunities can contribute to reducing economic disparities linked to caste.

9. **Future Outlook:**

- **Social Integration:** Continued efforts toward social integration and the dismantling of caste-based prejudices are essential for fostering a more cohesive and inclusive society.

- **Policy Reforms:** Ongoing policy reforms addressing educational, economic, and political disparities can contribute to long-term development by ensuring equal opportunities for all.

The caste system has had a profound impact on Indian society, influencing social structures, economic dynamics, and development opportunities. While legal reforms and affirmative action have aimed to address historical injustices, challenges persist in achieving true social equality and inclusivity. Ongoing efforts in education, economic empowerment, and social integration are crucial for building a more equitable and progressive society in India.

- Family structure and roles of men and women

Family Structure and Roles of Men and Women in Ancient Indian Society

1. **Joint Family System:**

- **Core Social Unit:** The joint family was the fundamental social unit in ancient India, comprising multiple generations living together. It emphasized familial bonds, shared responsibilities, and mutual support.

2. **Roles of Men:**

- **Breadwinners and Protectors:** Men were typically regarded as breadwinners and protectors of the family. Their primary responsibilities included providing for the family's economic needs and ensuring its safety.

- **Decision-Making Authority:** Men held decision-making authority within the family structure. Patriarchal norms guided familial governance, with the eldest male often assuming a leadership role.

- **Occupational Roles:** Occupational roles varied, with men engaging in diverse professions based on social class. While some were warriors or rulers, others worked in trade, agriculture, or artisanal occupations.

3. **Roles of Women:**

- **Home and Family Care:** Women's primary roles centered around home and family care. They managed household affairs, including cooking, cleaning, and raising children.

- **Cultural and Religious Duties:** Women played crucial roles in cultural and religious activities. They were responsible for passing down traditions, performing rituals, and contributing to the spiritual well-being of the family.

- **Craftsmanship:** In certain periods, women were involved in craftsmanship, particularly in creating textiles and handicrafts. Their skills contributed to both family sustenance and economic activities.

- **Educational Opportunities:** Educational opportunities for women varied. While some had access to education, particularly in affluent families, others faced restrictions.

4. Marriage and Family Dynamics:

- **Arranged Marriages:** Marriage was often arranged by families, with considerations including caste, social status, and economic factors. Arranged marriages aimed at fostering social cohesion and maintaining familial traditions.

- **Role in Family Ceremonies:** Women played central roles in family ceremonies, including weddings and religious rituals. Their active participation contributed to the continuity of cultural practices.

5. Children and Education:

- **Importance of Progeny:** The importance of progeny, particularly male heirs, was emphasized. Sons were seen as continuers of the family lineage and contributors to ancestral rites.

- **Educational Opportunities:** Educational opportunities for children were linked to social status. While some received formal education, others, especially in rural settings, learned practical skills within the family.

6. **Changing Roles Over Time:**

- **Evolving Socioeconomic Factors:** Socioeconomic factors influenced family structures and gender roles. Urbanization and economic shifts led to changing dynamics in occupational roles and educational opportunities for both men and women.

- **Impact of Social Reform Movements:** Social reform movements, particularly in the 19th and 20th centuries, advocated for women's education, legal rights, and an end to oppressive practices like child marriage and sati.

7. **Religious Influence:**

- **Diversity in Religious Practices:** Religious beliefs influenced family structures and roles. Different regions and communities had diverse practices, with variations in rituals, ceremonies, and the interpretation of religious texts.

8. **Challenges and Opportunities:**

- **Challenges Faced by Women:** Women faced challenges related to societal expectations, restricted educational opportunities, and limited decision-making authority. Practices like purdah further constrained women's social interactions.

- **Opportunities for Empowerment:** Over time, societal changes and legal reforms have provided opportunities for women's empowerment. Increased access to education and greater economic independence have contributed to evolving gender roles.

9. **Legacy and Contemporary Perspectives:**

- **Legacy of Family Values:** The legacy of family values, emphasizing unity, respect for elders, and collective well-being, continues to influence contemporary Indian families.

- **Changing Gender Dynamics:** Contemporary Indian society reflects changing gender dynamics, with increased emphasis on gender equality, educational opportunities for women, and evolving roles within the family.

The family structure in ancient India was rooted in the joint family system, with distinct roles for men and women. While men were primarily associated with economic responsibilities and decision-making, women played central roles in household management, cultural activities, and religious ceremonies. Historical changes, socio-economic shifts, and contemporary reforms have contributed to evolving gender roles and opportunities for both men and women in Indian society.

- **Clothing, Food, and Social Customs in Ancient Indian Society**

Ancient Indian society, known for its rich cultural tapestry, exhibited distinctive clothing, food practices, and social customs that were deeply intertwined with the region's diverse geography, climate, and cultural influences.

Clothing:

1. **Fabric and Styles:**

- **Diversity in Textiles:** India was renowned for its diverse textiles. Cotton, silk, and wool were commonly used. Different regions had distinct weaving traditions, resulting in a variety of fabrics, including fine muslin, silk brocade, and woolen textiles.

2. **Unisex Clothing:**

- **Similar Styles for Men and Women:** Traditional attire for both men and women often included draped garments. The dhoti for men and the saree for women were prevalent, showcasing a certain level of unisex clothing.

3. **Ornamentation and Accessories:**

- **Emphasis on Jewelry:** Ornamentation was a significant aspect of dressing. Both men and women adorned themselves with intricate jewelry, including necklaces, earrings, bracelets, and anklets. Precious metals like gold and gemstones were highly valued.

4. **Cultural Influence:**

- **Regional Variations:** Clothing styles varied across regions, reflecting local traditions and climatic conditions. The use of turbans, for example, was more common in the north, while southern regions favored different headgear.

5. **Symbolism in Attire:**

- **Social and Religious Significance:** Clothing often held social and religious symbolism. Certain colors, fabrics, and styles were associated with specific occasions, rituals, or social status.

Food:

1. Vegetarian Emphasis:

- **Prevalence of Vegetarianism:** Ancient Indian cuisine exhibited a strong emphasis on vegetarianism, influenced by religious beliefs such as Hinduism and Jainism. Grains, pulses, vegetables, and dairy products formed the core of the diet.

2. Spices and Flavors:

- **Rich Culinary Heritage:** Indian cuisine was characterized by its use of a wide array of spices, herbs, and flavors. The blending of aromatic spices, such as cumin, coriander, and cardamom, created intricate and flavorful dishes.

3. Regional Diversity:

- **Distinct Regional Cuisines:** Different regions developed unique culinary traditions based on local produce and cultural influences. The use of coconut and tamarind in southern cuisine, for instance, contrasted with the flavors of mustard and poppy seeds in eastern dishes.

4. Importance of Rituals:

- **Ritualistic Dining:** Dining was often a ritualistic and communal affair. Traditional practices, such as eating with one's hands, reflected cultural norms and were considered a more intimate and respectful way of consuming food.

5. **Ayurvedic Principles:**

- **Balancing Diet:** Ayurveda, the ancient Indian system of medicine, influenced dietary practices. The concept of balancing different tastes (sweet, salty, sour, bitter, pungent, and astringent) for overall well-being was integral to Ayurvedic principles.

Social Customs:

1. **Ceremonial Practices:**

- **Sacred Rites and Rituals:** Social customs were often intertwined with religious practices. Ceremonies, festivals, and rites of passage played a significant role, emphasizing the importance of community and familial ties.

2. **Hierarchy and Etiquette:**

- **Social Hierarchy:** Society had a hierarchical structure, influencing social customs and etiquette. Respect for elders, adherence to caste norms, and the recognition of social roles were fundamental aspects of social interactions.

3. **Guest Hospitality:**

- **Culture of Hospitality:** Hospitality towards guests was highly valued. Welcoming guests with warmth, offering refreshments, and ensuring their comfort were considered important social customs.

4. **Artistic and Literary Traditions:**

- **Expression Through Arts:** Social customs found expression in various art forms. Dance, music, and literature often depicted societal norms, values, and narratives, contributing to the preservation of cultural heritage.

5. **Egalitarian Values:**

- **Spiritual and Moral Teachings:** Philosophical and moral teachings from ancient texts emphasized egalitarian values, encouraging compassion, non-violence, and harmony in social interactions.

Ancient Indian society, marked by its cultural diversity and spiritual richness, found expression in the everyday lives of its people through distinctive clothing, food practices, and social customs. The intricate weaving of these elements contributed to the vibrant tapestry of India's cultural heritage.

-Examination of the status and roles of women in ancient Indian society.

In ancient Indian society, the status and roles of women were influenced by a complex interplay of cultural, religious, and social factors. While there was considerable diversity across regions and periods, certain overarching patterns can be observed.

Status:

Women in ancient India occupied multifaceted roles within the family and community. The prevailing social structure often assigned them distinct positions based on patriarchal norms. The Manusmriti, an ancient legal text, codified social roles and underscored the subordinate status of women. Despite this, the Rigveda, an ancient religious text, acknowledged the importance of women in domestic life and society.

Roles:

1. Family Responsibilities:

- Women played central roles in managing household affairs, including cooking, cleaning, and childcare. Their contributions were vital to the overall well-being of the family.

- Duties extended to participating in religious ceremonies, ensuring the continuity of cultural practices, and passing down traditions to subsequent generations.

2. Marriage and Motherhood:

- Marriage was considered a significant societal expectation, and women were often married at a young age. Arranged marriages were prevalent, with considerations such as caste, social status, and familial compatibility influencing the matchmaking process.

- Motherhood was highly valued, and the birth of sons, in particular, was considered auspicious. Sons were seen as continuers of the family lineage and contributors to ancestral rites.

3. Occupational Roles:

- While societal norms often limited women's participation in certain occupations, they did engage in various economic activities. Women were involved in crafts, weaving, and agricultural work, contributing to family sustenance.

- Certain texts, like the Arthashastra, acknowledged the

economic significance of women's participation in trade and commerce.

4. Education:

- Educational opportunities for women varied across social classes. In affluent families, some women received formal education, particularly in subjects like music, dance, and literature.

- However, access to education was limited for many, and the focus was often on practical skills necessary for managing a household.

5. Religious and Spiritual Roles:

- Women played active roles in religious ceremonies and rituals. They were responsible for maintaining domestic altars, performing daily rituals, and participating in community celebrations.

- The concept of 'Ardhangini,' signifying the wife as the other half of her husband, underscored the spiritual partnership within marital relationships.

6. Legal and Social Constraints:

- Legal codes like the Manusmriti articulated certain constraints on women's autonomy. Women were expected to be subservient to male authority figures, and restrictions on their freedom were codified.

- Sati, although not widespread in ancient times, did exist as a practice where widows self-immolated on their husband's funeral pyre. Over time, social reform movements sought to eradicate such practices.

7. Challenges and Empowerment:

- Women faced challenges related to societal expectations, restricted educational opportunities, and limited decision-making authority. Practices like purdah further constrained women's social interactions.

- Over time, social reform movements and evolving societal norms contributed to empowering women. Efforts to address issues like child marriage, dowry, and widowhood gained traction.

8. Literary and Artistic Contributions:

- Women made significant contributions to literature, arts, and philosophy. Prominent female poets like Andal and philosophers like Gargi Vachaknavi are celebrated in ancient texts for their intellectual prowess.

- The epics, Ramayana and Mahabharata, feature strong female characters like Sita and Draupadi, offering nuanced portrayals of women in ancient Indian society.

The status and roles of women in ancient Indian society were complex and multifaceted. While societal norms often prescribed certain limitations, women actively contributed to various aspects of family, economy, and culture. The historical context reveals both constraints and instances of empowerment, providing a nuanced understanding of women's roles in the rich tapestry of ancient Indian civilization.

- Analysis of women contributions to various fields, including literature, politics, and arts.

Women in ancient Indian society made substantial contributions across diverse fields, leaving a lasting impact on literature, politics, and the arts. These contributions, although often underrepresented in historical records, played a crucial role in shaping the cultural and intellectual landscape of the time.

Literature:

- **Poetry and Philosophy:** Women poets like Andal and Akka Mahadevi are celebrated for their profound contributions to devotional poetry. Gargi Vachaknavi, known for her philosophical insights, engaged in intellectual debates during Vedic times.

- **Epics and Narratives:** Female characters in epics like Sita and Draupadi provided nuanced portrayals, reflecting strength, resilience, and moral fortitude. Women contributed to oral storytelling traditions, preserving cultural narratives.

Politics:

- **Queens and Rulers:** Some women held influential political roles. Queen Didda of Kashmir and Razia Sultana, the only female ruler of the Delhi Sultanate, exemplify instances where women ascended to positions of political authority.

- **Advisors and Diplomats:** Women often served as advisors and diplomats, contributing to strategic decisions. Their roles were pivotal in maintaining diplomatic ties and fostering political stability.

Arts:

- **Dance and Music:** Women were integral to the world of performing arts. Classical dance forms, such as Bharatanatyam, owe much to historical female dancers. Musicians like Mira Bai, a saint and poet, enriched the cultural milieu with devotional songs.

- **Craftsmanship:** Women engaged in various crafts, including textile weaving and pottery. Their artistic expressions adorned homes and contributed to the economic prosperity of their communities.

Religious and Spiritual Contributions:

- **Spiritual Leaders:** Women played roles as spiritual leaders and gurus. Maitreyi and Gargi were revered for their philosophical wisdom. Mirabai's devotion to Lord Krishna and her devotional compositions are widely celebrated.

- **Monastic Traditions:** Some women chose a monastic life, contributing to the establishment of monastic institutions. The Bhikkhuni Sangha in Buddhism, for example, saw the participation of women in spiritual leadership.

Intellectual Contributions:

- **Philosophy and Debates:** Women engaged in intellectual debates and philosophical discussions. Gargi Vachaknavi's participation in debates with sage Yajnavalkya showcased intellectual prowess and a deep understanding of philosophical concepts.

Educational and Social Initiatives:

- **Patronage of Learning:** Wealthy and influential women often served as patrons of learning institutions, supporting scholars and educational endeavors.

- **Social Reforms:** Women were instrumental in social reform movements. Raja Ram Mohan Roy's mother, Tarini Devi, was an advocate for women's education and social reforms during the early 19th century.

Legacy:

- **Literary Heritage:** Women's contributions to literature left a significant literary legacy. Their poems, philosophical writings, and narratives continue to be studied and appreciated.

- **Cultural Influence:** Women contributed to the preservation and propagation of cultural practices, including rituals, festivals, and artistic traditions, shaping the cultural identity of their communities.

The contributions of women in ancient Indian society were diverse and multifaceted. While navigating societal norms and constraints, women actively participated in shaping literature, politics, and the arts. Their legacies endure, providing valuable insights into the richness of ancient Indian civilization and the role of women in its intellectual and cultural vibrancy.

- Factors that influenced women's empowerment and challenges they faced.

Women in ancient Indian society experienced a complex

interplay of factors that both influenced their empowerment and presented formidable challenges. The societal fabric of the time, shaped by cultural, religious, and economic dynamics, played a pivotal role in determining the status and agency of women.

Factors Influencing Women's Empowerment:

1. Educational Opportunities:

- **Affluent Families:** Women from affluent families had better access to education. Some received formal education in subjects like literature, music, and philosophy.

- **Cultural Centers:** Urban centers and cultural hubs became focal points for learning. Women engaged in intellectual pursuits, contributing to the dissemination of knowledge.

2. Philosophical and Religious Traditions:

- **Spiritual Leadership:** Certain religious traditions recognized women as spiritual leaders. Gargi Vachaknavi's engagement in philosophical debates and Mirabai's devotion exemplify women's roles in spiritual domains.

- **Inclusive Values:** The foundational philosophies of some sects emphasized the equality of all souls, fostering an environment where women could actively participate in religious and philosophical discourses.

3. Economic Independence:

- **Craftsmanship:** Women were actively involved in crafts such as weaving and pottery, contributing to economic activities. Their craftsmanship played a crucial role in sustaining families and communities.

- **Trade and Commerce:** In some regions, women engaged in trade and commerce, showcasing economic agency and contributing to the financial well-being of their households.

4. Political Roles:

- **Queens and Rulers:** Some women held political power. Queens like Didda of Kashmir and Razia Sultana of the Delhi Sultanate exemplify instances where women ascended to positions of political authority.

- **Advisors and Diplomats:** Women served as advisors and diplomats, actively participating in political decision-making and contributing to diplomatic endeavors.

5. Social Reform Movements:

- **Advocacy for Change:** Social reform movements, such as those led by Raja Ram Mohan Roy, sought to address societal issues. Women like Tarini Devi actively advocated for women's education and social reforms.

Challenges Faced by Women:

1. Patriarchal Social Structure:

- **Restricted Autonomy:** The prevalent patriarchal social structure limited women's autonomy. Legal codes like the Manusmriti codified restrictions, emphasizing the subordinate status of women.

- **Cultural Norms:** Cultural norms and expectations dictated societal roles, often confining women to specific spheres and reinforcing traditional gender roles.

2. Educational Constraints:

- **Limited Access:** Despite educational opportunities for some, many women faced restricted access to formal education. Educational disparities were often linked to social class and economic status.

- **Emphasis on Practical Skills:** The focus on practical skills for managing households sometimes overshadowed the importance of formal education for women.

3. Social Norms and Expectations:

- **Marriage and Family Expectations:** Social norms placed significant importance on marriage and family life. Arranged marriages and societal expectations often influenced women's life choices and aspirations.

- **Societal Judgments:** Women faced societal judgments based on adherence to cultural norms. Deviations from expected behavior could lead to social ostracism.

4. Legal Constraints:

- **Manusmriti Codes:** Legal codes, such as the Manusmriti, articulated constraints on women's autonomy and reinforced traditional gender norms. These legal frameworks perpetuated gender-based inequalities.

- **Limited Legal Rights:** Women had limited legal rights, and their ability to inherit property or participate in legal proceedings was often curtailed.

5. Cultural Practices:

- **Sati and Widowhood:** Sati, although not widespread in ancient times, did exist as a practice where widows self-immolated on their husband's funeral pyre. Widowhood brought societal challenges and limited opportunities for remarriage.

- **Purdah System:** Practices like purdah restricted women's social interactions and visibility outside the domestic sphere.

6. Resistance to Change:

- **Conservatism:** Societal conservatism and resistance to change hindered women's progress. Traditionalist views sometimes perpetuated discriminatory practices and restricted opportunities for women.

The empowerment of women in ancient Indian society was influenced by a complex interplay of factors. While some women found avenues for education, economic independence, and political participation, many faced formidable challenges rooted in patriarchal norms, legal constraints, and societal expectations. Understanding these historical dynamics provides insights into the intricate tapestry of women's roles and struggles in ancient India.

Chapter 11

Cultural Legacy and Contemporary Relevance

The cultural legacy of ancient Indian society has left an indelible mark on the contemporary landscape, influencing various facets of modern India. The enduring relevance of its traditions, philosophies, and artistic expressions is evident in numerous aspects of today's society.

Cultural Legacy:

1. Philosophical Wisdom:

- **Spiritual Philosophy:** The profound spiritual philosophies articulated in ancient texts, such as the Vedas, Upanishads, and Bhagavad Gita, continue to shape the spiritual outlook of millions. Concepts like dharma, karma, and moksha remain central to philosophical discourse.

2. Art and Architecture:

- **Architectural Marvels:** The architectural brilliance of ancient structures like the temples at Khajuraho, Ajanta, and Ellora reflects the artistic and engineering prowess of the time. These monuments stand as a testament to India's rich artistic heritage.

3. Literary Traditions:

- **Epics and Literature:** The epics, Ramayana and Mahabharata, and classical literature from ancient India continue to be celebrated. These narratives not only provide cultural and moral lessons but also serve as sources of inspiration for contemporary writers and artists.

4. Cultural Practices:

- **Festivals and Rituals:** Festivals like Diwali, Holi, and Navaratri have roots in ancient traditions. The celebratory spirit, rituals, and cultural practices associated with these festivals remain vibrant, fostering a sense of cultural continuity.

5. Yoga and Ayurveda:

- **Yoga Philosophy:** The ancient practice of yoga, rooted in spiritual and physical well-being, has gained global popularity. Its emphasis on mindfulness, meditation, and holistic health continues to resonate in contemporary wellness practices.

- **Ayurvedic Medicine:** Ayurveda, the traditional system of medicine, contributes to holistic health approaches. The emphasis on natural remedies, lifestyle balance, and individualized wellness aligns with modern trends in alternative medicine.

Contemporary Relevance:

1. Spiritual and Philosophical Influence:

- **Spiritual Diversity:** The diverse spiritual landscape of modern India draws from ancient philosophies. The coexistence of various spiritual traditions, including Hinduism, Buddhism, Jainism, and Sikhism, reflects the enduring pluralistic ethos.

2. Arts and Entertainment:

- **Classical Arts:** Classical dance forms like Bharatanatyam, Kathak, and Odissi thrive, connecting contemporary performers to ancient artistic traditions. The fusion of classical and contemporary styles in music and dance reflects a dynamic cultural evolution.

3. Cultural Festivals:

- **Celebration of Diversity:** Festivals rooted in ancient traditions celebrate India's cultural diversity. These celebrations, marked by vibrant colors, music, and rituals, foster a sense of unity and communal harmony.

4. Global Influence:

- **Yoga and Meditation:** The global popularity of yoga and meditation highlights the worldwide impact of ancient Indian practices. Yoga studios, meditation retreats, and mindfulness programs integrate these ancient techniques into modern lifestyles.

- **Indian Diaspora:** Communities in various parts of the world maintain and celebrate their Indian cultural identity, emphasizing the enduring global influence of ancient Indian traditions.

5. Cultural Revival and Preservation:

- **Cultural Institutions:** Efforts to preserve and promote cultural heritage are evident in the establishment of cultural institutions, museums, and research centers. These initiatives contribute to the documentation and revitalization of ancient cultural practices.

- **Revival of Traditional Arts:** Contemporary artists and scholars actively engage in reviving traditional art forms, ensuring their continuation and relevance in the modern era.

6. Ethical and Moral Values:

- **Moral Guidelines:** The ethical principles embedded in ancient texts, such as the concept of dharma, continue to guide ethical decision-making. These values provide a moral compass for individuals in various spheres of life.

- Modern reinterpretations of ancient art, music, and literature

- Continuing influence of ancient Indian philosophies

The profound philosophies that originated in ancient India continue to exert a profound and enduring influence on various aspects of contemporary life. These philosophical frameworks, deeply rooted in spirituality and ethical considerations, have transcended temporal boundaries, shaping the cultural, social, and intellectual landscape of modern India and beyond.

1. Spiritual Resonance:

The spiritual philosophies of Vedanta, Yoga, and Samkhya remain integral to the spiritual fabric of contemporary India. Individuals continue to seek spiritual fulfillment through practices like meditation, self-realization, and the exploration of higher consciousness, drawing directly from these ancient philosophical traditions.

2. Ethical Guidance:

Philosophical principles such as dharma, karma, and ahimsa provide ethical guidance in navigating moral dilemmas and ethical decision-making. These timeless values resonate in contemporary debates on social justice, environmental responsibility, and personal conduct.

3. Holistic Wellness Practices:

The holistic wellness approach embedded in Ayurveda, an ancient system of medicine, continues to influence contemporary health practices. The emphasis on balance, natural remedies, and preventive healthcare aligns with modern trends in holistic well-being.

4. Yoga as a Global Phenomenon:

The practice of Yoga, rooted in ancient philosophy, has transcended its cultural origins to become a global phenomenon. Yoga studios worldwide offer classes that integrate physical postures, breath control, and mindfulness, contributing to mental and physical well-being.

5. Mindfulness and Meditation:

The emphasis on mindfulness and meditation, inherent in ancient contemplative traditions, has gained widespread recognition for its positive impact on mental health. Mindfulness practices derived from ancient philosophies are incorporated into modern therapeutic interventions.

6. Social Justice and Inclusivity:

Philosophical ideals of equality and inclusivity, as seen in the teachings of saints and reformers like Kabir and Ravidas, continue to inspire movements for social justice. Advocacy for marginalized communities draws strength from these age-old principles.

7. Ecological Consciousness:

Ancient Indian philosophies, rooted in a deep connection with nature, contribute to contemporary discussions on environmentalism and sustainable living. The recognition of the interdependence of all living beings aligns with modern ecological consciousness.

8. Global Interfaith Dialogue:

The inclusive and pluralistic nature of certain ancient Indian philosophies facilitates global interfaith dialogue. The philosophy of Vasudhaiva Kutumbakam, considering the world as one family, resonates in discussions on global cooperation and understanding.

9. Modern Intellectual Discourse:

Philosophical debates on metaphysics, epistemology, and ethics from ancient Indian traditions continue to stimulate intellectual discussions. Scholars and thinkers engage with these timeless concepts, integrating them into contemporary discourse on philosophy and spirituality.

10. Integration in Education:

Educational institutions incorporate the study of ancient Indian philosophies, fostering a deeper understanding of cultural heritage. Academic programs explore the relevance of these philosophies in contemporary contexts, contributing to a well-rounded education.

In essence, the continuing influence of ancient Indian philosophies is a testament to their enduring wisdom and adaptability. As individuals and societies navigate the complexities of the modern world, these ancient philosophical traditions provide valuable insights and guidance, enriching lives with spiritual depth, ethical awareness, and a holistic approach to well-being.

- Exploration of the lasting impact of ancient Indian culture on modern India and the world.

The lasting impact of ancient Indian culture on modern India and the world is profound, touching upon diverse aspects of life, from philosophy and spirituality to art, science, and social structures. This enduring influence reflects the resilience and timelessness of the cultural legacy that has transcended centuries, shaping contemporary identities and global perspectives.

Philosophical Continuity:

Ancient Indian philosophy, with its deep spiritual roots, continues to resonate in modern India. Concepts such as dharma (moral duty), karma (action and its consequences), and moksha (liberation) provide a moral and spiritual framework that informs ethical decision-making and shapes individual and societal values. The philosophies of Vedanta, Samkhya, and Yoga, emphasizing self-realization and the pursuit of higher consciousness, contribute to the spiritual tapestry of the nation.

Cultural Diversity and Unity:

Ancient India's cultural diversity, evident in its languages, traditions, and rituals, remains a defining feature of modern India. The coexistence of various cultural practices, languages, and art forms fosters a sense of unity in diversity. Festivals like Diwali, Holi, and Eid showcase this cultural richness, serving as vibrant expressions of unity that transcend religious and regional boundaries.

Artistic Expressions:

The artistic traditions of ancient India have left an indelible mark on contemporary artistic expressions. Classical dance forms like Bharatanatyam, Odissi, and Kathak continue to thrive, connecting modern performers to the grace and storytelling techniques of their ancient counterparts. In painting, the intricate art of miniatures and the murals of Ajanta and Ellora inspire contemporary artists who blend traditional styles with modern sensibilities.

Architectural Marvels:

Architectural marvels from ancient India, such as the temples of Khajuraho and the intricately carved structures of Hampi, not only stand as testament to ancient engineering prowess but also serve as inspiration for modern architects. The fusion of traditional architectural styles with modern designs can be seen in contemporary structures that pay homage to the aesthetic brilliance of the past.

Yoga's Global Influence:

The ancient practice of Yoga, rooted in spiritual and physical well-being, has transcended its cultural origins to become a global phenomenon. Yoga studios around the world offer classes that integrate ancient postures, breathing techniques, and mindfulness, contributing to mental and physical wellness on a global scale.

Ayurveda and Holistic Health:

Ayurveda, the traditional system of medicine, continues to influence contemporary approaches to health and well-being. The emphasis on holistic wellness, personalized health plans, and natural remedies aligns with the growing global interest in alternative and complementary medicine.

Scientific and Mathematical Contributions:

Ancient Indian contributions to science and mathematics, including the concept of zero, the decimal system, and advancements in astronomy, resonate in modern scientific thought. The intellectual legacy of ancient scholars like Aryabhata and Brahmagupta continues to inspire contemporary scientists and mathematicians.

Social and Ethical Values:

The emphasis on social justice, compassion, and ethical living embedded in ancient Indian texts contributes to the ethical framework of modern Indian society. Concepts of non-violence (ahimsa) and compassion (karuna) find expression in social movements, advocacy for animal rights, and humanitarian efforts.

Literary Heritage:

The epics of Ramayana and Mahabharata, along with the philosophical dialogues in texts like Upanishads, continue to influence literary and artistic expressions. Contemporary authors draw inspiration from these ancient narratives, offering reinterpretations and exploring timeless themes that resonate with modern readers.

Global Cultural Exchange:

Ancient Indian culture serves as a bridge for global cultural exchange. The popularity of Indian cinema, literature, and performing arts on the international stage reflects the enduring fascination with the cultural richness that emanates from ancient traditions.

The lasting impact of ancient Indian culture on modern India and the world is multifaceted and profound. It is evident in the daily lives of individuals, the diverse cultural expressions, and the global recognition of India's intellectual and artistic contributions. As the nation continues to evolve, the cultural legacy from ancient times remains a source of inspiration, guiding contemporary society towards a harmonious synthesis of tradition and modernity.

- Analysis of how cultural elements continue to influence development policies, practices, and perspectives.

Cultural elements exert a significant influence on development policies, practices, and perspectives, shaping the trajectory of societal progress. This analysis explores how cultural factors continue to play a pivotal role in influencing and shaping various aspects of development.

Cultural Values and Development Goals:

Cultural values deeply embedded in societies often influence the prioritization of development goals. For example, societies with a strong emphasis on communal harmony may prioritize social welfare and inclusivity in their development policies, fostering a sense of collective well-being.

Education and Cultural Context:

Educational policies are profoundly impacted by cultural considerations. The content, language, and methods of education are often tailored to align with cultural norms and values. Respect for cultural diversity is increasingly recognized as an essential aspect of a well-rounded education.

Economic Practices and Traditional Industries:

Development policies often intersect with economic practices rooted in cultural traditions. Governments may formulate policies that support and promote traditional industries, recognizing their cultural significance and contribution to local economies. This approach ensures a balance between modernization and the preservation of cultural heritage.

Urban Planning and Cultural Identity:

In urban planning, consideration of cultural identity is crucial. Development policies that respect and preserve historical landmarks, traditional architecture, and cultural spaces contribute to maintaining a sense of identity and continuity for communities amidst rapid urbanization.

Healthcare and Cultural Beliefs:

Healthcare practices are deeply influenced by cultural beliefs and traditions. Development in the healthcare sector requires an understanding of cultural perceptions of health, illness, and treatment. Integrating traditional healing practices into modern healthcare systems can enhance accessibility and acceptance.

Environmental Policies and Cultural Respect:

Environmental policies often encounter cultural considerations, especially regarding sacred sites or practices tied to the land. Balancing conservation efforts with cultural respect ensures sustainable development that aligns with the values of the local population.

Gender Equality and Cultural Norms:

Cultural norms significantly impact the implementation of gender equality policies. Development strategies need to navigate cultural sensitivities, addressing gender disparities while respecting diverse cultural perspectives on gender roles and responsibilities.

Social Welfare Programs and Community Participation:

Development practices increasingly recognize the importance of community participation. Cultural elements play a crucial role in shaping community dynamics and engagement. Policies that acknowledge and leverage cultural networks and traditions often lead to more effective social welfare programs.

Technological Adoption and Cultural Adaptation:

The adoption of technology is influenced by cultural attitudes towards innovation and change. Development initiatives that consider cultural adaptation in technology adoption are more likely to be embraced and sustained by communities.

Globalization and Cultural Preservation:

Globalization brings both opportunities and challenges for cultural preservation. Development policies need to strike a balance between embracing global influences and safeguarding cultural heritage. Initiatives that promote cultural exchange without eroding local traditions contribute to sustainable development.

Cultural elements continue to be integral to the development landscape. Acknowledging and incorporating cultural nuances in policies and practices not only enhances the effectiveness of development initiatives but also fosters a more inclusive and sustainable approach to progress. It is through this nuanced understanding of cultural influences that development can be truly responsive to the diverse needs and aspirations of communities worldwide.

- Discussion of the importance of preserving and promoting ancient Indian cultural heritage.

Preserving and promoting ancient Indian cultural heritage is of paramount importance as it represents a reservoir of wisdom, identity, and inspiration that transcends generations. The rich tapestry of India's cultural heritage encompasses diverse elements, including art, literature, philosophy, and traditions, offering invaluable insights into the nation's history and contributing to a vibrant global cultural tapestry.

Preserving Historical Continuity:

Ancient Indian cultural heritage serves as a bridge connecting the past, present, and future. By preserving historical continuity, it provides a profound understanding of the roots from which contemporary India has grown. This sense of continuity fosters a collective identity and a shared cultural consciousness that strengthens societal bonds.

Transmission of Ethical Values:

The ethical and moral values embedded in ancient Indian cultural heritage provide a moral compass for contemporary society. Texts like the Bhagavad Gita and the Ramayana offer timeless lessons on righteousness, duty, and the pursuit of a virtuous life. Preserving these teachings is essential for imparting ethical guidance to future generations.

Cultural Diversity and Pluralism:

India's cultural heritage celebrates diversity and pluralism. It encapsulates a myriad of languages, art forms, music, dance, and traditions that vary across regions and communities.

Preserving this diversity ensures the continuation of a harmonious coexistence of different cultures, fostering a sense of unity in diversity.

Source of Artistic Inspiration:

Ancient Indian art forms, including sculpture, painting, and architecture, are reservoirs of artistic inspiration. Preserving these art forms not only maintains a connection with the past but also serves as a wellspring for contemporary artists. The fusion of traditional artistic techniques with modern expressions contributes to a dynamic cultural landscape.

Philosophical Wisdom for Modern Challenges:

The philosophical wisdom enshrined in ancient texts offers profound insights into the human experience and the challenges of life. Concepts such as yoga, meditation, and the pursuit of knowledge remain relevant in addressing modern-day stress, mental health issues, and the quest for meaning and purpose.

Tourism and Cultural Economy:

Preserving ancient cultural heritage contributes significantly to the tourism industry. Historical sites, temples, and cultural landmarks attract visitors from around the world, promoting cultural exchange and economic growth. Sustainable tourism, guided by a commitment to heritage conservation, ensures that these sites remain accessible for future generations.

Global Soft Power:

Ancient Indian cultural heritage enhances India's soft power on the global stage. The international recognition of practices like yoga and Ayurveda, rooted in ancient traditions, showcases India's cultural contributions to the world. Promoting and preserving these elements bolster India's global image as a repository of timeless wisdom.

Cultural Diplomacy and Understanding:

Cultural heritage serves as a powerful tool for diplomacy and fostering understanding between nations. By showcasing India's rich cultural heritage, diplomatic efforts can transcend political boundaries, fostering mutual respect and collaboration. Cultural exchange programs build bridges and promote a shared appreciation of humanity's cultural diversity.

Interconnectedness of Traditions:

Preserving ancient Indian cultural heritage contributes to the global narrative of interconnectedness. Many philosophical and scientific principles from ancient India resonate with global thought, emphasizing the universality of human experiences. This interconnectedness fosters a sense of shared heritage that transcends geographical boundaries.

The preservation and promotion of ancient Indian cultural heritage are essential for maintaining a strong sense of identity, fostering ethical values, and contributing to global cultural discourse. By safeguarding this heritage, India not only honors its past but also ensures that the rich tapestry of its cultural legacy continues to weave threads of inspiration and wisdom into the fabric of the present and the future.

- Examination of lessons that can be drawn from ancient Indian culture for sustainable development.

Ancient Indian culture offers profound lessons that resonate with the principles of sustainable development. These lessons, rooted in a holistic understanding of life and interconnectedness, provide valuable insights for shaping contemporary approaches to development that prioritize environmental stewardship, social equity, and economic well-being.

1. Harmony with Nature:

Ancient Indian culture emphasizes the interconnectedness between humans and nature. The concept of 'Vasudhaiva Kutumbakam,' viewing the world as one family, underscores the importance of living in harmony with the environment. Sustainable development requires recognizing and respecting nature's limits, preserving biodiversity, and adopting eco-friendly practices.

2. Circular Economy Principles:

Traditional Indian practices embody elements of a circular economy. Reincarnation, a central tenet in Hindu philosophy, aligns with the idea of recycling and reusing resources. Applying similar principles to modern economic systems encourages reducing waste, recycling materials, and designing products with end-of-life considerations.

3. Agricultural Wisdom:

Ancient agricultural practices in India, such as rainwater harvesting, crop rotation, and organic farming, are aligned with sustainable agriculture principles. Learning from these practices can inform contemporary agriculture, emphasizing regenerative farming methods, biodiversity conservation, and resilient food systems.

4. Water Conservation Techniques:

Ancient Indian cultures excelled in water conservation techniques, as seen in structures like stepwells. Incorporating such traditional water management practices into contemporary urban planning and agriculture can contribute to sustainable water use and mitigate the impact of water scarcity.

5. Mindful Consumption:

The philosophy of moderation and mindfulness, evident in practices like Ayurveda, encourages a balanced and sustainable approach to consumption. Applying these principles to modern lifestyles involves conscious choices, reducing waste, and embracing sustainable products and practices.

6. Social Inclusivity:

Ancient Indian cultures recognized the importance of social inclusivity and community welfare. Sustainable development must prioritize social equity, ensuring that economic benefits, educational opportunities, and healthcare services are accessible to all segments of society, thereby fostering inclusive growth.

7. Education for Sustainable Living:

Traditional education systems in ancient India, including Gurukuls, focused not only on academic knowledge but also on holistic development. Integrating modern education with values that promote sustainability, environmental awareness, and ethical responsibility can shape a more conscientious and responsible citizenry.

8. Non-violence and Compassion:

The principles of non-violence (ahimsa) and compassion, integral to Indian philosophy, resonate with the need for ethical and humane practices in all aspects of life, including business, governance, and interpersonal relationships. These values contribute to creating a sustainable and empathetic society.

9. Indigenous Knowledge Integration:

Ancient Indian cultures possess indigenous knowledge about medicinal plants, traditional building techniques, and local resource management. Integrating this indigenous wisdom into contemporary sustainable development strategies ensures that local contexts and traditional practices are considered.

10. Holistic Well-being:

The emphasis on holistic well-being in ancient Indian practices like Yoga extends beyond physical health to encompass mental, emotional, and spiritual wellness. Sustainable development should prioritize the well-being of individuals and communities, recognizing that true progress is measured by improvements in overall quality of life.

The lessons drawn from ancient Indian culture offer a blueprint for sustainable development that prioritizes environmental stewardship, social inclusivity, and holistic well-being. By integrating these timeless principles into contemporary practices, societies can move towards a more sustainable and resilient future, fostering a harmonious coexistence with nature and promoting the well-being of present and future generations.

Glossary

1. **Sacred Space:**

- **Definition:** A place designated for religious or spiritual activities, often characterized by specific architectural features conducive to worship.

2. **Iconography:**

- **Definition:** The visual representation of symbols and images in art, especially within a religious context, conveying specific meanings and messages.

3. **Ritualistic Function:**

- **Definition:** The designed functionality of religious art and architecture to accommodate and enhance religious ceremonies and rituals.

4. **Cultural Identity:**

- **Definition:** The identification with and expression of the unique cultural characteristics, including religious beliefs, of a particular group or community.

5. **Icon:**

- **Definition:** A religious image or representation, often depicting a deity, saint, or sacred person, venerated in religious traditions.

6. Commemoration:

- **Definition:** The act of remembering and honoring significant religious events, figures, or milestones through artistic means, such as paintings or sculptures.

7. Inspirational Source:

- **Definition:** The role of religious art and architecture as a source of inspiration, evoking spiritual and emotional responses from believers and admirers.

8. Architectural Landmark:

- **Definition:** A significant, easily recognizable architectural structure that serves as a prominent feature in a city or region, often associated with religious buildings.

9. Iconic Landmark:

- **Definition:** A distinctive and widely recognized landmark, often associated with religious structures, contributing to the identity and visual appeal of a location.

10. Interplay with Rituals:

- **Definition:** The dynamic interaction between the design elements of religious spaces and the rituals performed within them, enhancing the overall religious experience.

11. Sacred Art:

- **Definition:** Artistic expressions, including paintings, sculptures, and artifacts, created with the primary purpose of representing and honoring religious themes and beliefs.

12. Theology:

- **Definition:** The study of the nature of the divine, religious beliefs, and the practice of worship, influencing the themes and concepts depicted in religious art.

13. Architectural Symbolism:

- **Definition:** The use of architectural elements to convey specific meanings or ideas related to religious beliefs, traditions, and cultural identity.

14. Cultural Continuity:

- **Definition:** The concept of preserving and transmitting cultural and religious traditions across generations, often reflected in religious art and architectural forms.

15. Spiritual Narrative:

- **Definition:** The visual storytelling within religious art, conveying narratives related to spiritual beliefs, religious figures, and mythologies.

ABOUT THE AUTHOR

Dr Pawan Kumar Singh is currently working as Assistant Professor in the department of Ancient History and Culture at Mahatma Jyotiba Phule Rohilkhand University Campus Bareilly.

The educational qualification of the author is M.A. Ancient History, UGC Net and Ph.D. The Title of his research topic is "Prachin bhartiya kala mein Lakshmi avm uske vividh swaroopon ka ankan: Ek vishleshanatmak adhdhayan. His research paper has been published in various national and international research journal. He has also written editorial in various newspapers. The author is a renowned expert on ancient Indian Art, Indian religion, and philosophy.

The author is a permanent member of the UP-History Congress. He has successfully performed various administrative tasks of the university. At present, he is successfully directing the work of Proctor, NSS officer and assistant warden in the Hostel.
The Author has also served as vice president of Rohilkhand University Teachers Association.

www.ingramcontent.com/pod-product-compliance
Lightning Source LLC
LaVergne TN
LVHW041155150826
845673LV00001B/170

* 9 7 9 8 8 9 5 8 8 1 9 6 5 *